Why He Married Her & Played Me

The Sequel

PRESENTED BY

P. Koffe Brown

This book is written for informational purposes only. It contains general relationship information. This book is designed to assist with building healthy, strong, long-lasting relationships. It is the thoughts, personal and professional opinions of the Authors. Destined for Greatness Publishing Group and the Anthologist/Author disclaim any responsibility for actions taken without first seeking professional advice or for misunderstandings on the part of the reader.

D. F. G. Publishing House LLC

Printed in the United States of America

ISBN: 978-0-578-89219-1

Book Design by P. Koffe Brown & Yasmin M. Brown

Please enjoy our first publication titled "The Race to the Ring, The Seven Seas of a Successful Courtship."

"Why He Married Her and Played Me, Nine Secrets to What He's Thinking."

"A Date with Destiny, I Gotta Have Him Although I'm Married to You."

Be on the lookout for our next book coming Summer 2021

"She Chose Him & Screwed Me! Nine Reasons for Her Decision".

CONTENTS

ACKNOWLEDGEMENTS

I want to thank you, the reader, for picking up this book and enjoying the pages. If it were not for you, then writing for me would be in vain. I certainly want to thank God for blessing me with this unique idea to bring the value of healthy relationships to the forefront of all our minds. Next, I must thank **LOVE** for leading me to have a desire to share this type of connection with another human being. I also must thank my parents for creating me and showing me the power of loving one human being for life! I have never seen two people fight so hard to lead a life that shows the magic of partnership, purpose, patience, persistence, and passion. You two are a real-life example that all things are possible in a relationship if you believe!

I would also like to thank the humans that I have created Myles, Maya, and Yasmin Mone't. The three of you push me to win. Thank you for being my children and my reason **WHY**! You guys are making me into a "**DOPE**

BILLIONAIRE MOM." I enjoy being your mother. It has made me a much better woman. I love you, and always remember that you are my greatest gift!

Finally, I would be remised if I did not thank the other contributing authors and the fantastic editor on this project. As I began to think and consider the pages of this book, your names came to mind. For some reason beyond my understanding, you said YES without hesitation. For this, your time and your talent, I thank you. It is a great honor to share the stage and these pages with your presence. Again, thank you to my readers. May this book grace your life and bless your relationships forever. Enjoy dears welcome to the SEQUEL!!

P.S. Thank you to Mr. Wil Brown, III, who was the one man that pushed me into purpose and made me understand the importance of pursuing my passion no matter what it cost! Thank you for being a great father to our children and being an arrow to help point them in the right direction! They are becoming all that we said that they would be.

Rest peacefully. Sunrise February 14, 1967, to Sunset July 09, 2011.

Love Is...

Love is the one power that can transform all our lives. Love can create an environment that makes us come alive and be at ease. Love is a shelter from the rain of life. Love is past a feeling into purpose. Love leads and guides us into truth. Love covers all our human faults, frailties, and failures. Love outlasts anything and everything in life. Love does not know the grave; it remembers those who captured our hearts that no longer dwell here. Love is the master of meaning. Love is the passion that drives us to the arms of one another. Love is pure, purposeful, and painless. Love is the magic that reveals the meaning of why we choose one person over the other. Love is the perfect thing on earth. Love leads us to our purposed person and commands our undivided attention. Love arrests our hearts while captivating our minds. Love is the energy that wakes us up in the morning, and it is the same force that lays us peacefully to sleep at night. Love never fails. Love never changes. Love is consistent. Love is contagious. Love is captivating and calming. Love is beauty beyond one's body. Love is what we need to enjoy a perfectly imperfect person. Love is what brings a smile to our face while we dance away the night. Love is the laughter that we share while lying in each other's arms. Love is the exchange of spirit while connected to the soul of our commanded partner. We do not need love; we are LOVE because God created us, and He is LOVE. Love is EVERYTHING!

Welcome to "Why He Married Her & Played Me. The Sequel"

Introduction

Often in my journey through relational life, I find people that have had this not so exciting experience—being involved with someone from an intimate perspective only to find that you are not the only one. Not knowing that there is competition in the eyes of your man can be the ultimate wedge that drives you apart. "Why He Married Her & Played Me" is here to help you change all of that. Knowing these nine secrets to his decision can equip you with the information that you need so that you never get played again!

By playing, I mean that you will be aware of what is going on by the actions that he displays and not only the words that he speaks. No longer will you walk around with the relationship vail of trust covering your face. You will have the power to know the man that you are dealing with. There is nothing more powerful than being in the "know"! As you read through these pages and learn from these amazing men, be sure to have your highlighters ready, honey, as there are some stellar messages that you do not want to forget!

This book is designed as a game-changer, truth bringer, and eye-opener! We will share tools with you that will not only stop the negative experience but enlighten, inspire, and educate you in your quest to identify your purposed person. Please join me as we take the journey to "Why He Married Her & Played Me, The Sequel" ……

Much love, peace, and respect to all the leading ladies!

Coach Koffe

Coach P. Koffe Brown - Anthologist Visionary, CEO & Marketing Guru

What's the love of your life? For the speaker, certified life coach, and healing practitioner, P. Koffe Brown, it's empowering others to heal.

A proponent for living life with passion and purpose, Koffe's story is not much different from most of her clients. With astounding clarity borne from years of intensive work, Koffe has unraveled the impact of freedom in her life and recognized that her life's purpose revolves around supporting others in their journey to inner peace, wholeness, and love.

Koffe's combination of personal experience and professional skills compelled her to create ***Destined for Greatness PAS*** in 2003. Through inspirational speaking and coaching, Koffe takes clients on a transformational journey of healing and growth, all to incorporate a holistic approach to soul cleansing and deliberate change. She focuses on shifting relationship patterns, raising self-awareness, and channeling energies back to its true essence, one of divine spiritual love.

Driven by her mission to promote holistic growth, Koffe creates unique, powerful, and high energy experiences that delight others to take hold of their vision and put it into action. Embodying the essence of her core message, "Free your mind, and the past will soon be left behind!" Koffe contentedly fulfills her passion for serving others through coaching, writing, workshops, social media talk shows & live seminars.

An author, avid reader, lover of communication, and all things transformative, Koffe's mission is - and will forever be - to heal, inspire, and create change in the world, one heart at a time.

NATURAL

From the Poetic Genius herself, The Leading Lady Coach P. Koffe Brown….

September 05, 2018

Dear Future, I mean, Dear NOW!

Not only am I grateful that you found me, but I am also thankful that I knew to **CHOOSE YOU**! See, we all have freedom of choice, and I admit my choices have not always been Divinely Orchestrated. My **FLESH** made my decisions in times past, which left me going in cycles, vicious ones at that. Before you came, I decided to **DIE** to the decisions that brought harm to me as a **WOMAN**. I could no longer live outside while bleeding to death internally. You see, your **ATTRACTION** to me was not just because of my bouncy booty, big breast, brown eyes, gracious smile, and the way I sashay your way. You saw the God in me, the oil from my being crushed into **PURITY**! You saw a **DIAMOND** who had gone through

FIRE to burn away all the filth from who I used to be. You saw a fighter who was not afraid to get in the ring and box with the enemy who wants to destroy humanity! You know you found me because it was time for **FAVOUR** to chase you down and you to be all that you could be for **GOD'S GLORY**! So, I choose you, a man after God's heart for me! People will be confused and dumbfounded when they find out that we walk together, equally yoked, and agree that no one or nothing comes before *God, the US, and our family*! I honor you, Sir, with my body, I respect your authority, and I stand beside you for as long as there is air in my lungs to breathe! Dear, **NOW** you have the absolute best of me!"

Signed a Queen Positioned,

P. Koffe Brown

Contributing Author
Dr. Adrian M. Woods

Adrian M. Woods EdD. is a writer, poet, counselor, veteran, and educator. He holds five collegiate degrees, including a master's and Doctorate in education from the University of Houston Clearlake. He has a certification in counseling and mediation. Even with his credentials, he considers his greatest success as being a husband and father. He uses his unique and tragic experiences to explore and articulate life mysteries to help others navigate their own trials and tribulations.

CHAPTER ONE

There's More to Sex than Missionary Position

With
Dr. Adrian Woods

Before I begin to delve into this delicate topic, I would like to preface by stating that no one, married nor single, should be forced to engage in any activity against their will. Consenting adults should only perform sexual intercourse of any form or fashion.

The conversation of sex can be a sensitive topic to bring up. Various factors influence sensitivity to the subject, such as age, personal experiences, faith, personal moral code, etc. Many have suffered through the emotional trauma that prevents the ability to embrace a sexual nature. You may not always understand a person's view on sex, but you should be able to look beyond your own selfish desires to respect their viewpoints. Despite modern dogma, sex is a selfless act. You must be able to give yourself entirely to that person showing your most vulnerable sides. Even though the word submits is seen as a negative in modern times, a woman must be willing to consent to be penetrated and submit to a man. If you are unable to give yourself to a person completely, there will always be struggles.

According to a study by Scott, Roades, etc., the most commonly reported major contributing factors for divorce were a lack of commitment, frequent infidelity, and conflict/arguing. One of the primary reasons people felt that divorce was the only answer was infidelity. More participants blamed their partners than blamed themselves for the divorce. Women felt men were greedy, immature, or unloving because they felt the need to satisfy their urges with another woman. A study by Crystal Raypool stated that the number one reason men cheat is unmet sexual needs.

Personal experience has shown me that despite the statistics, many females prefer to hold off on any sexual conversations until they have gotten to know a suitor on a deeper level. I have heard the phrase, "There's more to life than sex." or "I want to be seen for more than my body." Many feel that a more profound connection will allow clearer thoughts that will enable an individual to make a more educated and mature decision about the relationship. You see the person as they are without the fog of sexual euphoria. Women are looking at the subject through sunglasses blinded by the X chromosome.

"A person's sex drive refers to a hypothetical construct encompassing one's attitudes toward sex, sexual desires, and sexual behaviors" (Baumeister, 2000). Statistically, men have a much stronger sex drive than women. Most men think about sex at least once a day, while only a quarter of women admit to thinking about it that frequently. Women feel that the trials and tribulations of life supersede any form of sexual desire as daily life stresses build, their passion for sexual interactions decreases. Women think that men should understand and accept the lack of sex because they care for them. Women don't see this for what it is, a form of emotional abuse. A relationship is emotionally abusive when there is a consistent pattern of offensive words and neglective behaviors that wear down a person's self-esteem and undermine their mental health.

For men, sex is like the police banging at the door because someone called 911 and claims there is a burglar in the residence armed with a machete and a nuclear missile. The poison in our veins called testosterone drives our bodies to crave the warmth and the physicality of human contact. It is often a thirst that, without being quenched, devours your thoughts, emotions, and happiness. No amount of intimacy or love takes away that thirst. Like a vampire craves the taste of life-giving blood to sustain, as does a man desire sex. No, a man will not die due to lack of sex, but they will be left feeling unappreciated, unloved, and unvalued. This causes an emotional disconnection because a woman's site causes a chain reaction that shoots impulses from our brains that electrify our nerves that cause the muscles to relax, allowing blood to flow in and fill our manhood, causing an erection.

I know I used many colorful languages to say sex for men is a need and not a want. According to the Miriam-Webster dictionary, a want is "a desire for something or a possession." While a need is a physiological or psychological requirement for the well-being of an organism. And that is what women need to understand when dealing with a man's sexuality. Men require sex to feel loved, invigorated, and happy. Sex for men begins as a hunger. The hormones build in our system and drive us to pursue sustenance. When the desire is fed, a man is more focused, confident, mentally ready for the daily grind's pressure and stress.

I already know that many females ready this are rolling their eyes and thinking, "It is not that serious." I am here to tell you that it is that serious. Denying a man's physical intimacy is a blow to their pride. And just lying there letting him have his way with you is not sufficient enough. The more exciting and passionate the sex, the more energetic and willing to fulfill their responsibilities as providers and helpmates.

Ladies, I am not telling you to give up the cookie on the first night. Every woman should have standards. A man should be worthy of your precious gift. I learned my game from both my mother and my grandfather. I believe two different viewpoints taught me to appreciate a woman, their body, and their mind. My mother always told me that it is a man's job to chase and a woman's job to be attainable. Attainable does not mean give it up to every Tom, Dick, or Harry that compliments you, shows you attention, or waves a few funky dollars in front of you. People put energy and time into what they value, and a woman should be valued more than any treasure.

My grandfather taught me that the way to any woman's heart and body is through the mind. Where the mind goes, the body follows. My grandfather had a way with ladies that I feel is unexplainable. He would smile and compliment any woman who ran across his path, regardless of appearance, color, or class. He also made a funny statement or asked them about their day. He would listen and comment to make sure they felt heard. Unlike many people in today's world, my grandfather was genuine. He wanted each woman to walk away from an encounter with him feeling uniquely special.

When a man presents himself in a deserving manner, and you decide to bless him with your time and body, you are taking responsibility for his sexual hunger. If you want to continue to be his primary focus, you must learn how to soothe the savage beast. If you know that a man desires sex several times a week, and you are not comfortable enough to fulfill this need, please understand that this may not be the man for you. Ladies, you do not want your time wasted, so please respect his. A man naturally has a wandering eye. As much as women think they can control this, you can't. In a world where sex is on every television screen, accessible on everyone's phone, and literally on the countless number of street corners worldwide, you must be the focal point of his desire.

I understand the world is harsh. There are days when you are drained and feel beat down, but you still need to support his needs. Ladies, the little things do matter. Everyone harbors a personal fetish. A fetish is a desire that is based on abnormal circumstances. A fetish can be various things from a particular situation, a piece of clothing, or a specific body part. Sex therapist Dr. Rajan Bhosle states, "Sexual fetishes are nothing more than unconventional, yet harmless sexual practices. People need to understand that having a fetish doesn't make you weird of a pervert. They just must be nurtured within set boundaries and limitations. If he favors a specific feature on you, put on an outfit that does justice to this feature and obtains his gaze as you walk by. For example, if your man likes feet, you should make sure your feet are pedicured and ready to present. On the day you may be tired, but your partner requires the attention of sexual gratification, maybe let him wash your feet or ask him to paint your toes while you relax. This way, both your needs are met. Your need to relax and his hunger is given a snack.

And yes, ladies, sometimes you are just going to give up that cookie. Hopefully, you find pleasure or gratification by pleasing your man. There will be times when he needs to be one with you and ease the tension. There is nothing worse to a man than when he works, helps with the kids, and tries to spend time with his mate only to be rejected. Experts state that one sign of a loveless relationship is sex less than once a month. This is why communication and compromise are essential. As soon as you see a man as your potential partner, the conversation of sex needs to be had. It needs to sneak in there with the discussion about plans, finances, and kids. If your man wants it six times a week, but you are good with two, meet in the middle at three or four. Once again, if you are unwilling to compromise or feel whatever you give him should be enough, you are a likely candidate to be cheated on. A man can find a woman that meets all of his criteria except for sex, and he will still let her go for a partner that meets a few of them but knocks his socks off in the bedroom. Yes, men are that basic. That is why I stated that sex for men is a need.

Life is not a fairytale, and men are not mind readers, so women have to communicate their expectations when it comes to sex effectively. The whole ideology of him needing to explore your body and finding your hidden erogenous zones is romantic literary nonsense. To you, there are more important things in life, and if you hold on tightly to this way of thinking, poppa will be a rolling stone. Every man believes he is a beast in the bed, so he wants to please you. Tell him where to touch, where to kiss, or even what you want to be smacked, flipped, or rubbed down. This will boost his ego and provide a more satisfying sexual experience for both of you.

And ladies, just as people grow and change; so, do a man's sexual desires. As young men, we are more likely to be sowing our wild oats, as my grandmother would call it. I still hear her telling me to stop chasing after those girls, and all I think about is humping like a jackrabbit. As a man ages, he appreciates his life mate's dedication to him and his family. Most men find a woman caring for his child sexier. Getting out of the shower, bending over in a pair of shorts cleaning the room, or being kind enough to make us a plate after a long day can turn into sexual energy.

This no longer the medieval times where the pure and virginal bride is preferred. Men want a sexually confident woman and into him and the act of sex as he is. We have all heard the term lady in the streets and freak in the sheets. You need to hone the craft of sex. Do not be afraid to experiment with different techniques. Do your research, talk to your girlfriends, and yes, maybe view pornographic videos and take what you learned to your man. Your man will be shocked and grateful for your desire to please him.

Ladies, I know this may be a lot to take in. This statement is true; the one who controls the cookie controls the world. I started this conversation by stating that no one should have to have sexual intercourse with anyone against their will. That is your body, ladies. You choose what to and what not to do with it. But if you want to be someone's spouse and ensure a long healthy marriage, you need to choose someone you are sexually compatible with. I will leave you with a statement that we have all heard, "what you won't do, the lady down the street will."

References

12, C. K. on J. (2020, June 12). Are You in a Loveless Marriage? 23 Possible Red Flags. Relish. https://hellorelish.com/articles/loveless-marriage-red-flags.html.

Gordon, S. (2020, September 17). How to Identify and Cope With Emotional Abuse. Verywell Mind. https://www.verywellmind.com/identify-and-cope-with-emotional-abuse-4156673.

Raypole, C. (2019, October 11). Why Do People Cheat in Relationships. Healthline.com. https://www.healthline.com/health/why-people-cheat.

Scott, S. B., Rhoades, G. K., Stanley, S. M., Allen, E. S., & Markman, H. J. (2013). Reasons for divorce and recollections of premarital intervention: Implications for improving relationship education. Couple and Family

Psychology: Research and Practice, 2(2), 131–145. https://doi.org/10.1037/a0032025

The Times of India. (2017, March 6). 8 common sexual fetishes - Times of India. The Times of India. https://timesofindia.indiatimes.com/life-style/relationships/love-sex/8-common-sexual-fetishes/articleshow/9923062.cms#:~:text=A%20fetish%20is%20characterised%20as,Sex%20expert%20Dr.&
;text=One%20should%20understand%20that%20having,nurture%20them%20within%20set%20limits.

Watson, L. J. (2017, August 12). The Truth About Men and Sex. Psychology Today. https://www.psychologytoday.com/us/blog/married-and-still-doing-it/201708/the-truth-about-men-and-sex.

Contributing Author
Christopher A. Pratcher

Defining myself has never been easy. I am a person still figuring out life. I would first like to start by highlighting my faith in Christ because, without my God, who strengthens me, I would be so much less. With that said, I am a proud husband and equally proud father of six children.

I have led a career primarily in sales and have even ventured out to start my very own business(es). I am currently working on eCommerce websites and leaving a legacy for my family. I am a first-time author on a fantastic project which I hope transcends into more possibilities to inspire, change and uplift.

CHAPTER TWO

You Need a Daddy, Not a Man

With
Chris Pratcher

I found myself sitting there wondering why she was so insecure when I didn't give the reason. You often wonder why people react or are the way they are with you. But in reality, it's not just you.

See, her norm was that when everything was good, it was a problem, and when things were dysfunctional, that seemed normal. When daddy issues are present and let me add that it's not always a "her" issue. But because you fight him at the first sign of what looks like he may be a tad bit disconnected, it leaves him wanting actually to disconnect. Nah, he just wanted a little wind-down time. To him, it's called "me time," but to her, it's "you want to do you time."

In her mind, that looks like, "oh, he thinks he's slick," but he wants a bit of breathing room in actuality. Time apart helps a man with a good woman realize that there isn't much good inventory, so he will be right back. Your suffocation isn't what is going to keep him.

All he wanted to do was have you trust him. Avoiding his concerns because that's what you are used to doing is not the way to build a solid relationship. Dismissiveness and avoidance often come into play when you feel like you can't trust. Anything that looks eerily familiar to distrust, abandonment, or something that doesn't make you feel secure, you run.

These types of issues can manifest in so many ways and often don't come to light until it's too late or there has been a series of relationships that have ended almost precisely the same way. If you find yourself getting insecure or feeling abandoned in everyday situations.

There are instances where the dad may have been there physically. However, they were disrespected, weren't shown love in the home, or had any regard for. In these types of instances, what happens is that the woman may begin to mimic what she saw as a child. It may be a means of protection before the anticipated hurt comes, or it is just a way to express the inside's anger. Let me be clear; daddy issues are not just a female term. It is a general term for attachment issues that can affect both males and females.

Let me start by saying this. I would like us to stop shaming women and using the term "daddy issues" in a demeaning way that insults women whose fathers failed and they had no control over.

- Was dad present? Yes or No?
- Was dad absent? Yes, No, or Kinda
- Was he there physically but emotionally unavailable? Yes or No?

- Was he abusive? Yes or No?

The term Daddy issues come off as unfavorable and could be taken as an attack on her character. Plainly put, the average person in a relationship addressing someone about their daddy issues is damn near fighting words.

Some of the tell-tale signs of someone who is having these types of experiences are

- You are anxious when your partner is not around.
- You have a tough time trusting others (which a lot of us do)
- You feel insecure about intimacy and often avoid anything that requires getting in touch with who you are or your past.

We must tread lightly when we're talking about or want to address this. Depending upon how committed you are to making the relationship work, this will need to be discussed and worked through either with your partner or with a professional therapist.

Some questions you can ask yourself to sift through any baggage or emotional trauma you may have/had surrounded by your caregiver are:

- What patterns keep popping up in all my relationships?
- Are the relationships ending in a similar manner or because of the same thing?
- Have I taken a deep look into the relationship, if any, that I had with my father?

If being alone scares you and you find yourself bouncing from one relationship to the next, what tends to happen is you leave no room or time for you to discover your own identity. It thwarts you from moving forward in a fulfilling relationship because the fear becomes so big and active in your life, it becomes the compass that you live by.

Preferring to stay in a dysfunctional dynamic is also a sign that there may be some underlying issues, as stated previously, but we will unpack a little bit here. When someone comes along and is operating in normalcy, that can throw up a false red flag that something must be wrong. Then comes the temptation to sabotage or "start something" because not being toxic, fighting, and consistently enjoying yourself is not customary in your eyes. Cause Guuuurrrlll, that is not normal.

This leads us to the excessive need to be reassured that your partner loves you and needs you. Now, this can be exhausting to the person trying to love you correctly. Man, look, all these questions can leave a guy questioning you at this point. I mean, now he has questions

- Is everything okay with you because I'm good?

- Are you trying to convince yourself that you want to be in this relationship?
- Why don't you trust that I'm where I say that I am or who I say I'm with?

To be held to a standard of constantly having to let you know that there is nothing negative happening with the relationship, checking in and letting you know they love you, and tiptoeing around your feelings to avoid any confrontation will come off needy and can push them away.

Loving you will start to feel like a job and not something seamless and fluid. Don't allow this society of social media to make you think it's okay to be toxic or "I may be a little crazy, but I have a good heart" is cute. I mean, I do like a little crazy with my eggs. Buuuttt is not attractive, and several things need to be unpacked with that type of thinking.

Let's talk a little about sex:

There is absolutely nothing wrong with having a healthy appetite for sex. A lot of men appreciate a partner who's into sex just as much as he is. Now, where it becomes a problem is when your esteem is solely based on whether someone wants you sexually. Sometimes feeling attractive and adored by others sexually is a warped way of thinking or makes you feel incredibly close to being loved. The need to be attached by any means necessary is unhealthy, but we will not trace that back to our childhood or connect the relationship we lacked or had with our dads.

Constantly worrying if your partner will leave you because you're jealous, overprotective, or clingy means you have an anxious attachment. If you're tempted to check cell phones, spy, and smell his drawers to ensure they're not cheating, you will also run your dude into the hills. When these relationships end, you never take any ownership of why it didn't work and then move on to the next one and keep repeating the same pattern.

- What unresolved grievances do you have with either of your parents?
- Is there a specific memory that you can account for where you felt unsafe and abandoned? When was it and how old were you?

I wanted to make this chapter as interactive as possible because as we read, a lot of times, it's just that. We don't take the time to pause, think and write down our thoughts. When we write down our thoughts, it allows us to reflect and get in touch with what's going on.

We've talked about being clingy and overprotective. What about being dismissive and avoiding any and almost all closeness? Fear of being close and being vulnerable can also be rooted back in your childhood. Anytime you find yourself running or perhaps putting up a wall for an excellent partner to come through and grow, that's a sign it's some unresolved issues. It subconsciously reminds you of the pain you may have experienced, and you want no parts of it. It often comes out like, "The last time I trusted someone like that, I got hurt." So, then you go into a shell and become hardened against everything. One thing to remember is that it is okay to start the new person with 100% and not 0% trust.

Being too independent can also hurt your relationship as well. The "I don't need a man" mentality can make it difficult for the man to define himself in your life that wants to take care of you and be there for you. However, because you may have had an absent dad and witnessed your mom doing and making it happen all on her own makes you feel this way. You may have heard while growing up from the women your life, "You don't need a man" or "We don't need him; we make it happen all on our own." Don't you want to feel needed and respected in your role in your partner's life? Yes, of course! Why would anyone want to be settled with someone who is constantly reminded in words or actions they aren't needed? Now resentment settles in because you may feel like they aren't pulling their weight. Know what? You're right; they can't because you're pulling it all.

While this is a safe method and keeps you from experiencing any hurt, on the flip side, it also keeps you from experiencing any joy that love has to offer. It would help if you decided on how you're going to move forward healthily.

Healing

I will end this chapter with some encouragement on where to start the healing process. I think the best start is to start with your past, no matter how painful it is. Next, seek some help or advice from a trusted confidant who can give you good counsel. You cannot continue to surround yourself with people who have a trauma bond with you.

When you surround yourself with people who have the same dysfunctional value system sentiments as you related to love and relationship, it'll keep you in that loop.

If you desire a loving and healthy relationship, why don't you start having a loving and healthy relationship with yourself first? After all, we know that if we have a warped sense of esteem or self-image, it'll cause us to view everyone else with a lens that may not be the truth. Our standards begin to get unreasonable as we keep bouncing from relationship to relationship.

- What makes you feel safe in a relationship?
- What is the very first thing that attracts you to your partner? Think about the very first couple of things? Why?

I'm not suggesting that everyone needs therapy. Wait, yes, I am. We all need someone to talk to. But you don't have to succumb to terrible relationships and a life full of heartache because you weren't afforded a great relationship with your dad. You didn't have a choice in the matter. What you do have a choice in is how you decide you're going to move forward. You can choose not to be defined by any childhood trauma you may have experienced. Going back is painful. Remembering often takes us to a place where we're reliving how bad our dads may have done us.

We need a relationship. You need a relationship, even if it's not romantic, you cannot do this alone, and the good news is you're not. There are so many ways for us to heal, but the first step is acknowledgment.

Let's talk about forgiveness. Why don't you take the time to forgive your parents or specifically your dad for how he may not have shown up in your life. You have to start setting boundaries in your thought life when this hot topic comes up in your mind. If this is a place of pain, you have to contain it and ensure it's not spilling over everything else in your life as it has in the past. You must push past WITHOUT the apology. Release that person from whatever they did. Release yourself from how you may have given it a pass to damage some things in your life. It goes deep. When we can start to discover WHEN we're operating in 'daddy issues", that's when we can start putting those actions in their place. You can begin to isolate any negative experiences in your relationship instead of throwing it all away when things aren't going in the right direction.

Remember, you are the common denominator.

If you are a believer, let your validation start coming from God. It boils down to that we're looking for things in our partner that they can't fulfill. This is going to take some soul-searching conversations with God. Yes, you can honor the partner in your life without feeling like you're losing who you are. Yes, you can be vulnerable and feminine without being imbalanced in your need to be needed.

Healthy and consistent relationships are possible on the road to healing. Understanding your role in how they play out is so necessary. I hope what we've discussed in this chapter sets you up to become more aware of your role in all of your relationships, begin the road to healing and gain the healthy relationship you desire!

Contributing Author
Leonard Davies

From humble beginnings and life of the ordinary kind emerges a human soul that seeks to make whole people's kindness from all walks of life. Leonard has accomplished a great deal on planet earth, from saving the lives of displaced refugees in Africa to protecting the theater's warfighter. In a small way giving hope and contributing to what makes us impeccable as decent human beings.

Leonard believes life is what you make it, and being outrageously persistent gives you as an individual the absolute belief that nothing is impossible when you focus your mind on accomplishing your goals. Living a simple life and doing the most to help others has always been a driving force behind his life approach. Making a difference and leaving a mark on whatever you do in life can change others' thought processes on the receiving end. And therein starts the chain of events of giving back and elevating the thought process of making an ordinary life and exemplary life.

Our imperfections sometimes blind our vision to see ourselves in a better place than where we started. Life is a journey on a long road of obstacles and trails. We will fall nine times but get up ten. Never give up. Adapt, Evolve and Persevere. Always be kind to others and know that the universe always gives back two folds when you never expect it. It's better to change the narrative than to be an afterthought. Being loudest in a space doesn't make you fill the room. Move in silence and be relentless. Live, Love and Laugh always. Dream big, and the manifestation of your humble soul will reign forever. Peace and Love!

CHAPTER THREE

You Want Me to Provide What???

(Gold Digging)

With
Leonard Davies

Welcome to my point of view and thoughts on this beautiful topic. It's a delight and honor to share my humble reflections on the idea of "Gold Diggers." Before plunging into the abyss of the obvious, I would like to take you on a journey of the origins and experiences that formulated my thought process. A constructive viewpoint usually allows an idea's premise to be honestly challenged on its merits or lack thereof. In my opinion, with all the influencers present, "Gold Diggers" have the Nerve and the Audacity of the Ask with no remorse beholden to their core. How we see ourselves daily while discovering one's self-worth invites the constant battle that takes us through the pressures of whether to value what matters to us selfishly or what others have worked tirelessly to achieve.

In my humble opinion, many facets lead to the diminishing greed of folks' non-standards to want, feel, act, and look relevant. The Audacity of their minds and boldness of their Ask is never a wonder because the outrageous always makes the follow up a mere act of buffoonery. Knowing that life is hard, and not everyone is born with the advantages of a wealthy parent(s) or a trust fund does not give credence to the unwanted pressure to be relevant or act the part. And unfortunately, many fall prey to the intrigue chasing the noise and missing the signals.

My viewpoint of a "Gold Digger" cuts both ways related to a woman and a man. And the origins of the lunacy and the Ask originate from different perspectives based on what we have experience in our upbringing. The Want, the Need, the Desire to possess what is entirely out of reach is a natural human drive that makes us build determination to achieve the impossible. There is a distinct difference between achieving that and willfully using and abusing the kindness of one's core as a free pass to your materialistic orgasm. Some folks who come from nothing never had anything and don't work for something feel they can take whatever they want to make themselves feel good. At the same time, being relevant to society promotes glamour and materialistic riches and negates the means of getting by without putting in any efforts to achieve it all. The quick fix and the ridiculous request seem to be the order of our day. Understanding the environment of being without and not having much is the essence of what one can aspire to build on to make things achievable and affordable in their own lives. The lack of a fundamental premise to being content and working hard for what is desired cannot be understated in any way, shape, or form. It's the ideal of what we are and who we want to become.

Creating this space for immediate power and influence made other bystanders eager and long to be one. Being relevant or somewhat rich is wholly lost in the daily chatter's idea but settling for greed irrespective of how labor-intensive achieving such wealth and fortune can reveal seems to be the prevalent norm. Digging for Gold is not a pleasurable, fun experience, but it can be gratifying when those nuggets are discovered. As much as Gold is relevant and highly sought after, getting it differs in several ways. Gold enthusiasts would venture out on whatever process to experience the joy of finding something rewarding, which could enrich them beyond their wildest dreams. Now with having some details and background to this Golding Digging experience, let's embark on a journey to how this relates to our everyday current lives.

How it starts… From the beginning, the have nots have predominantly been looked upon in society as the unfortunate casualty of life and unfortunate geographical catastrophic alignments. There is always this frown from the community on how we look, how we dress, and how we are represented. With the constant pressures building, our minds sometimes cave into the ruthless narrative that you must gain wealth or relevance by any means necessary. We all know that there is a right way and a wrong way. The pressure never ends and, we, to our core, must understand to leverage the feeling of want versus a need. We are constantly reminded of what we see daily and how our neighbors make us feel when we step out of our dwellings. When the foundation of what matters is lost on the soul, we tend to drift to instant gratification, and nothing else matters. With selfish greed in hand, we feel that the masking fits disguising our ill-conceived actions. Pushing the narrative that somebody else's earning must somehow be at your disposal because your superficial needs are a matter of importance is brazenly reckless. It doesn't help social media platforms encourage and promote glitz and glamour, which adds to our daily life pressures. Aspiring to be something we are not while creating the importance of our selfish greed is a nuisance to our priorities. It comes down to our merchandising branding gods that make the folks in the poorest of neighborhoods want to wear a pair of Balenciaga shoes when they can't pronounce the name, nor can their parents afford it. And the story goes on with the Christian Louboutin's, Gucci, Tom Ford, Marc Jacobs, and Prada's of the world. Lights, Camera, let me get mine Action.

Understanding your worth puts you in the frame of mind that others will envy. It elevates your mind and thought process of how you see value in yourself. It's not always about what you have and the elaborate presentation of your collection of wealth. Formulating what is essential to you allows you to understand what is critical and cheapen your brand, which is your name.

Making the distinction of the false narrative is crucial, and I think we need to visit that thought process as we journey together. If you are flaunting that you are wealthy and are willing to use discretionary funds to get your worldly pleasures fulfilled, you basically would have removed yourself from the list of individuals that get preyed on by so-called "Gold Diggers." That is all on that individual that is trying to get someone's panties or boxers off. That is, you in every way telegraphing your desires and what you are willing to give for it. You can't have your cake and eat it too. In this case, the Gold is readily available, and there is a Task for the Ask and Retrieval of it. The decision is by choice and understanding of the adults in said space. Moving along….

The thought process of the Ask and the Nerve of it is a story for the ages. The boldness and the rare guts to ask for the unimaginable will come at you with quickness and sudden shock. It usually starts with the inclination to have earned income, carry yourself decently, portray sophistication slightly above the average man or woman.

Your appearance doesn't look like you are homeless or without a job. You look like you have "money" in layman's terms. It's like you are being studied with no emphasis but your mere looks and their impression of you. He or she will move around with no indication that the Ask is being planned or they are about to get the intrusive shock of the moment. Naivete!!!!

Acquaintance is made, and then he/she is asked where you would like to go for dinner… With all the choices available and in reach, the most expensive restaurant is suggested. The backstory here is that he or she has never eaten at said place, nor will they probably ever eat there on their own, and factually they can't afford it, period. At dinner, since the prices are listed, the most expensive meal is ordered, and so is the 20-year-old bottle of wine on the menu. Never having consumed a $200.00 dinner plate before and never drank a $600.00 bottle of anything before this dinner outing. But it gets better, just like fine wine.

And the mere suggestion of the ask "would you like anything else"? Response: Yes. Knowing that there is a kid's menu with the most expensive meal selection topping at $50.00, you end up with a take-home tab of $300.00 and nothing off the kid's menu. On the way to the car, "oh sweetheart, my gas is low. Do you have any cash?" "Sure, how much would you like?" "I need gas for the week. $300 will do because my drive is a distance."

That's a dinner date… at $1,650.00

The Nerve and the Ask. You want me to do what?

Acquaintance is cemented, and as the conversation trends, one discovers that there is Galleria nearby, and it would be nice if they could do a little shopping. The invite is extended, and the tagalong is in place. The backstory here is that they own many pairs of shoes and fashionable clothing, notwithstanding no brand name period. In their words, the most spent on shoes is $100.00 easily. With the question asked, "would you like anything"? $1500.00 later and three pairs of Italian shoes never owned or purchased before—three pairs of jeans $500.00 and 2 pairs of Nikes at $600.00. The response at the moment is, "I might as well make use of this opportunity for me. Babe, I need a Harley so that I can get around the city quickly. I see that you have one, and it looks incredible. "

That's a $2600.00 tab on shoes and clothing; not forget the $20,000.00 for the Harley.

The Nerve and the Ask. You want me to do what?

Acquaintance is established and with the backdrop of a request or favor asked of at every meeting. Vacations and weekend getaways come up over chats. The backstory here is that one of the two individuals has never had a break, flown on a plane, or stayed at a hotel ever. Surprisingly when asked if they wanted to go somewhere for vacation for a few days, the response was "Yes." One said, let's go to Florida, knowing that the other had never traveled before and wanted to ease them into that lifestyle.

Response: No, I think not Florida is not all that honey; let's go to the Maldives and stay at the Radisson Blu Maldives. $1500 a night for five nights plus airfare. But why the Maldives? Response: "That's the kind of place I would love to hang out sounds perfect to me."

The tab instantly became a $10,000.00 Ask. Woooooosaaaaah

The Nerve and the Ask. You want me to do what?

Early acquaintance and the birthday is 72 hours away. The backstory here is akin to affection to bags, purses, and all things fashion. There are purses in that closet for sure, but there is not one item that carries a price tag of more than $200.00. On the way back from dinner in the cozy 745 massaging seats, the question is asked... What bag/purse would you like for your birthday? Response: "I was just about to ask where is my gift? Since you asked, I would like a, you know, a Louis Vuitton Tribute Patchwork Bag." Wait what? You want me to get you what? You make 35k a year while going to school part-time, but you just asked me to purchase you a 45,000.00 bag? Response: "Yes, I need it. I am worth it."

That was a $45,000.00 Ask with some Audacity spiced with the Nerve of it all.

The Nerve and the Ask. You want me to do what?

There is no logical or sensible explanation to these outlandish Ask in every scenario. There is neither a value trend nor self-worth exhibited in any instance. Asking for something that you know you can't afford as a want versus a need that matters less to your livelihood is beyond the pale. Many folks out there will ask for a handout at every turn, but this is ridiculous on every level. They will have the means and income and doing well but still feel that using someone for what they are worth is money in the bank any day. It's that instant gratification and need to be seen with something of value. My friends will see I have the new $300.00 Jordan's, but I can't keep a steady job. Or

I can walk around the block with a Birkin bag that costs $7,500, but you can't produce $50.00 saved in your bank account. Lost perspectives.

We live in a society that makes you believe that being regular is not cool, but being glamorous is the order of the day that makes for poor judgment in what matters. Unfortunately, all this drives this sad ill-gotten narrative even further, causing some people to believe that you must use others to get by and be relevant. Some will be pretty comfortable with having the man or woman purchase luxury gifts at their request and repeating the scheme with multiple people at the same time to gauge how much they can get for themselves. To put that simply, it's Gold Digging".

The mission always mystifies the mind and all the sound judgment one can plunder. The predetermination to get what they can and be honestly bold in acquiring the outrageous Ask is savagery and greed at its fullest. "Gold

Diggers" will stop at nothing to bleed you dry and tell the world how they got what they wanted and all the while scoping the next prey. The Ask and the Nerve of it have gotten much more sophisticated and elusive. But I can assure you that the blemishes left in their paths will always magnify the error in their ways and the power of discernment in their future victims.

I have seen and experienced every form of the Nerve to Ask and the plot to execute it flawlessly in my lifetime. When you are sincere and operate with a clear mind, you tend to be naïve sometimes in the spirit of being kind. When you get your Gold dug up, and you discover the Audacity of the Ask, you start plotting the beginning to current, meanwhile filling in the oddities of the moment. When you explore someone's mind, you see the subliminal messages of kindness, meanness, selfishness, love, and humility. You engage the unknown to connect with the present, and therein lies the key to acceptance and judgment of who they are in the flesh. There is nothing wrong with being kind and helping someone experience a side of life you have lived and make them see what else is there in the world of love and kindness. The ruthless pressure society imposes on us to be relevant by any means necessary is a culture that, unfortunately, is prevalent and destructive. Sometimes you will have to step back and see users' advancement and how they are unbothered by getting whatever they can out of you. Remember, "Gold Diggers" don't necessarily have to get a big score or grand take away. The approach is strategic and disguised with a pretense of interest and self-aggrandizement. Keep your mind's eye open because it will decipher the fallacious Ask and the Audacity of it when the Nerve emerges. At which time, allow your inner voice to project a sincere unapologetic response in the rawest and unfiltered form.

"YOU ASK ME TO DO WHAT"?

"I am sorry, come again!!!" Remember, all that glitters is not Gold, and Silver does shine bright! Peace and Love!

Contributing Author Jason Thibodeaux

Jason Thibodeaux, a native of Houston, TX, grew up knowing that he wanted to be an entertainer starting at a young age. As Jason grew, so did his personality. It often sparked interest and had him in the spotlight. He has performed in high school and college marching bands. Jason has also engineered for stage productions and film. He stepped out of the background and into the forefront, where he has given awe-inspiring and emotionally jarring performances.

Jason has been featured in several films as well as stage productions such as **"The Sons We Were Meant to Be," "A Right to Preach," "Christmas with the In-Laws, Parts I and II," "Retribution," "Do's and Don'ts of Dating,"** and **"VI the Series"** written and directed by some of Houston's finest writers and directors. He starred in the feature film **"Can You Hear Me"** and directed and starred in **"Pawns."** He helped write the feature film "**Karma,**" in which he made a cameo appearance. Jason became a published author penning a chapter in the book **"The Race to the Ring, The Seven C's to a Successful Relationship."** He recently completed another chapter in the soon-to-be best-selling **"Why He Married Her & Played Me, The Sequel."** Jason's resume continues to grow due to his strong integrity and drive, and he hasn't shown signs of slowing down!

For more information and book, visit:

IMDBPro JasonThibodeax (II)

CHAPTER FOUR

Lower Your Voice, Please!

With
Jason Thibodeaux

When you first hear this statement, a lot of thoughts probably run through your mind. Wait, "is she loud talking him??" "Is he raising his voice at her??" "Is that person just naturally loud??" Again, a lot of things come to mind. However, this isn't a book on any subject; W*hy He Married Her & Played Me, The Sequel,* right?? So, let's get busy!!

What are the reasons this chapter has importance? Are you wondering why you're just so passionate about your relationships, but the man you're dating at the moment never seems to be as passionate as you? Does he seem unattached? I get it, you just "LOVE" hard, and he needs to respect your feelings. Well, you are correct. He does need to respect your feelings, but are your feelings the only ones that need respect? I ask this because I have had many relationships in my life. Some business, but most were romantic if we even made it that far. Now, I am not going to portray myself as a relationship guru by any means. Still, I have been in enough relationships and have spoken with enough men and women about relationships to determine what I want and do not want, what I like and do not like, and most importantly, what I will accept and will not accept. All of these are important when considering a spouse, and one should not take precedence over another.

Ladies, let me ask an honest question…… Since this is a book, and you are most likely not in front of anyone (or at least holding a conversation with anyone while reading), why do you think you are getting your point across while speaking loudly or yelling at your man?? Do you think you are winning the argument?? Do you genuinely believe you are that passionate about your point while grabbing air and clapping your hands in his face??? Go ahead and answer truthfully… I bet at least 90% of you will admit (if you are truthful) that you are more into your perception of winning the argument than actually making a valid point while speaking loudly at your man. Go ahead, be honest. Can I be honest?? Most likely, you won the argument because your man doesn't feel the need to prove you wrong, feel like yelling back, doesn't want to get physical with you seeing it is a losing battle on our end if the law gets involved, or just doesn't care at that point. So, congrats on winning an argument that he may not have cared about in the first place. Then you are probably wondering why he is so distant, and other women catch his attention. This scenario becomes more prevalent the older we get, and at some point, we as men don't care how fine you are; just don't bring your drama our way.

Have you ever wondered how a lady that is not as cute, shapely, or has their stuff together got the man to marry her but play you? Have you ever thought that men are just scared or intimidated by you and chose to date someone lower than your level of accomplishment? Think your strong independence threatens them? Ever wonder if these men just don't like being belittled by your successes or feel that they are not needed or desired by your overwhelming independence that you constantly let him know you have??? If you are a successful lady, congratulations. Most men love a successful woman. We desire it. We just don't want to be emasculated if you just so happen to make more than we do. Think about it for a moment......

If you find yourself having the desire to disrespect your man by putting him in check often, then he may not be the man for you. If you were more equally yoked, you shouldn't have to correct his behavior. Especially not publicly. Have you found yourself being that woman that has to be loud, get attention, let everyone know you're the "Baddest B" around, and no one better mess with you or your man? Public service announcement, you just helped yourself get played. Now your man has become prey to the other ladies around, and now you are seen as the weaker person because you felt the need to claim your man/property or, as I like to call it, "pee on your tree." The more you show out in private, the more likely your man is to get tired of your antics and choose to play in the streets. If you find yourself showing out in public, you are, in essence, pushing your man to play in the streets and invite other ladies into your relationship. Why?? Women love challenges and usually want what they can't have. It's more of a human trait than just a feature ladies possess; however, now they see him being disrespected and now want to play on your court, with your man, to see if they can steal him away from you! Most likely, he is seen as a victim of an unappreciative lady, and the new lady will vow to make it all better. Remember, it's easier to woo someone with honey instead of bitterness. Men go where they are appreciated, not always where we are needed. We naturally want to feel needed but will always go where we are appreciated.

Where is the Volume Coming From??

Let's get to the root of the matter. Most people raise their voices when they feel they are not being heard. They do it to get your attention when there is a problem. The real question in this instance is, why do you feel that you are not heard? What is the message that your partner is missing? Is it that you are not being listened to, or are you not getting the response you are looking for? When we feel that we are not getting the response from our partner that we are looking for, it is human nature to react in a manner that we think will get our partner's attention. Usually, this response is an increase in volume in hopes of getting noticed. The problem with this action is most of the time, our partner will respond with a high volume as well, in defense, which starts the process of both spouses not listening. Once either partner is no longer listening, the conversation is over!! It's time to lower your voice and possibly try communicating again after tempers have subsided.

Tone Deaf

Another form of needing to lower your volume has nothing to do with volume at all. It's something that I have challenges with myself. That's right!!! Mr. Perfect is not so perfect!!! Duh!! No one is truly perfect. The part of communication that I am referring to is tone. I have battled with tonal challenges my entire life. I come from two strong-minded, strong-willed parents that both had strong tones. I take after my father more regarding attitude, and ironically, that would be the parent with the more assertive manner. I'm speaking of a tone so strong that it could make children cry if they got angry. My father didn't have to yell for him to let you know you were treading on thin ice and were about to be in trouble. This is in no way speaking negatively of my father or my parents, and no, I did not come from a family with an abusive relationship. I am speaking to strengths and weaknesses and dictating how we maneuver challenges in life and relationships. You're probably wondering where I am going with this.... It's simple.

A firm tone works great when rearing children, dealing with other strong-minded individuals (mostly work situations), acting (LOL), etc. It does not generally work well in personal relationships. I say this because having a solid tone can be a blessing and a curse!! The benefit is, as stated above, when you need someone to leave you alone, a firm tone is an excellent warning to others that you are not in the mood to play. The style is a curse when you deal with someone that is sensitive to tone or may have low self-confidence, as it is easy to hurt their feelings and have them shut down on you while trying to communicate. I have found that most ladies I have been in relationships with are tone sensitive. Hell, I'm tone and volume sensitive myself and have no issues expressing that! When I am trying to have a complex discussion, and my wife raises her voice (when I feel the problem was not that big), I get hypersensitive and try to lower her voice. She usually wants me to change my tone. See what happens here??? We have to be careful how we communicate regularly as my wife naturally speaks loudly and has tonal challenges.

Are Your Constant Reminders Necessary!!

Please keep in mind that speaking loudly to someone does not always have to do with volume or even tone. You can push someone away by constantly nagging, constantly reminding him that you "really" don't need him. Constantly reminding him that you are making all of the money in the household and "holding him down." I know you frequently hear about men being beat down by the world, right? Well, it is true. We constantly get reminded of what we do and don't do correctly daily. Not only at work but by media, social media, etc., just to come home and have the lady we care about tell us what a real man should be doing for her to feel special. A lot of times, this from a lady who may have a fantasy/movie man in mind because she had not grown up with a father in the home. So…… Who made the checklist of a real man or what a real man should be providing to prove his love to you?

Most men work themselves to the bone to provide amenities for you, and often if kids are involved, them too. Is it a must that you rely on him to provide help with lights, running water, a working car to get back and forth to work? NO!! But he probably has his own vehicle to keep gassed up and running. He doesn't have to go out in the hot or freezing elements to put gas in your car. But most likely, he does. Now I know that most ladies reading this are saying what about me being beat down at work, gender discrimination, etc. That's all true, and yes, you ladies do deal with a lot as well, but that is not what this book is about now, is it? It is why men choose another woman over you and why you get the short end of the stick.

Your Silence is Deafening!!!!!

Ever heard the saying, even in silence, you are speaking loudly?? This is mainly used when social injustice happens, and one group will not speak up against the wrongdoings of their own. Their silence on these matters is deafening. The same goes for relationships. Just because you are not yelling does not mean you are not speaking loudly. A stare, a grunt, talking under your breath can all be deafening. Even from across the room. Energy!!! It's felt even when the person you care about is not near, correct? Well, the man you are dating doesn't just feel your positive energy from across the world; he feels the negative too. When you are silent productive communication is not happening. The issues are not being resolved, and most of the time, they are being exacerbated with the extra thoughts that come to mind during the silence. Be careful with using silence as your means of communication. You may think you are not saying anything, but you are sending a message loud and clear! Silence usually sends a message of not caring or not caring enough to speak on the matter.

Effects of Emotional Loudness

Last but not least, let's talk about feelings and emotions for a moment. I usually hear women describe men as soft these days, and in some instances, that is true. After all, most likely, a woman raised him with no stable male influence….. Stings, don't it?? Men (traditional men) are usually raised not to show emotion when upset; they channel most emotions inward until they have some form of an outburst. If you're lucky, said outburst would be verbal and not physical. One should not consider their man weak or play on these emotions because it is just childish for one and two; it can be perilous depending on that man's upbringing or experiences.

Imagine your man was raised in an abusive environment, which does happen more often than not in these modern times. Chances are they were taught to bottle their anger as not to trigger their parent's abusive actions. Those emotions will stay bottled up until he reaches a boiling point, and he finds himself in a situation where he can no longer channel that feeling safely and positively. By raising your voice at your man, you could quickly become that trigger that I was referring to earlier, creating a situation where you are now the target of his release of anger that was pinned up for many years. This is highly dangerous as he may seriously harm you and never meant to do anything outside of getting you out of his face or getting away from you. This becomes heightened if you are the type of woman that likes to get in the man's personal space and put your hands and fingers all in his face, clapping your hands at him, daring him to respond. This will not turn out well for him, and it will not turn out well for you!!!!

Now, let's look at the other side of the spectrum. What if your man was raised to express his emotions regularly? He is most likely a little more feminine acting than the first guy. Now you see him as a pansy or soft because he IS positively expressing himself. He talks more, is more emotional, and more sensitive. You still have a man that has a hard time channeling their emotions, just on the complete opposite end of the other side of the spectrum. Now you have outstanding men sitting in the house all day and paying someone to cut the yard, fix the sink, or just do things that were considered manly in the past. This man you feel you can disrespect whenever you want because of the way he expresses his feelings. Why is he a topic when he is already more sensitive than the first guy?? Men who attempt to express themselves and get disrespected and shut off tend to shut down and channel those emotions within. The danger here becomes similar to the first guy with one exception; this man wants to talk about his feelings and does not know how to suppress those feelings.

Again, this can lead to you placing yourself in a dangerous situation. With the constant expression of how much you feel he is soft; he may feel the need to prove to you how much of a man he really is.

In short, the gist of this whole chapter is straightforward, be mindful of how you treat the person you're dating. This chapter is not meant to beat down any ladies or men. This chapter is about how you communicate with the person you're dating and whether you are constantly nagging or disrespectful. If you find yourself being this person, then that is probably a good reason the man you love is now seeking attention from; or worse, married to someone else, and you were played!!

Contributing Author
DeCorey Hale

DeCorey Hale was born in the city of Sylacauga, Alabama, 30 minutes south of Birmingham. After graduation from high school, he attended Alabama State University, majoring in Sales and Marketing.

There, he was given a quality education, but he was equipped with skills that he still utilizes today. DeCorey is a known multitasker, often referring to it as "his gift and his curse." Though his life is as hectic as it is, he still makes time for those close to him and needs him.

Even though there are many hats that he currently wears, his first passion has always been writing. In 2014, DeCorey began blogging and freelancing for magazines such as Hip-Hop Album Debate, Xkluziv, and London LeBlanc. He grabbed the attention of many readers, eventually becoming a regular writer for the Huffington Post.

In 2015, DeCorey decided to revisit a story he was writing for his daughter, Nylah, named Ebenezer the Sneezer. This was his first book, released in 2017. While writing and networking with other blossoming entrepreneurs in 2015, he co-founded a beard care company, HIM BY DNA

When he is not writing, he is heavily involved in the local community, serving on several city boards, committees, and non-profits. He also enjoys offering a helping hand to fellow up-and-coming entrepreneurs.

CHAPTER FIVE

You Are a Freak in the Sheets, But Not a Lady in the Streets

I Can Lay with You, but Not Stay with You!

With
DeCorey Hale

I fully understand what the title of this book is, as well as my chapter. No, I am not married, nor have I ever been. I am, in fact, single as can be. This makes my text a lot more authentic as I speak it. You are a freak in the sheets but not a lady in the streets. In layman's terms, I can lay with you, but I cannot stay with you. At first glance, this rhetoric seems pretty harsh, and I can see why that is. But speaking from a single perspective, I can honestly say there are several reasons this may be. You've done just about everything that "serious" couples do. You've traveled together, hung out with each other's friends, and maybe even met each other's families. But despite all this, you're still stuck in that limbo between relationship and courtship. Although there are several reasons, he might not want to commit to a relationship fully, it will be one of two things; it's him, not you, or it is you, not him. Let us unpack this "situationship" and see exactly what's what shall we?

It Is Fun

Friends with benefits, just friends, kicking it. However, you want to label it, it's not serious. Coming from a male's perspective, the idea of having a woman that will cater to his every whim and not ask to be seen or ask for much more attention than in the sheets is fun. To him, it's a game. How long can he string her along with this? How does he tell her it's over once he's bored? Is she starting to care for him? These are logical questions; unfortunately, in the fun phase, they will never get answered. It is all about the moment. Sure, they enjoy each other, but to a certain extent. In his mind, the moment it becomes a relationship, the fun disappears, and now it becomes work. Now, relationships are work, but they should also be fun for sure. But because he may only be looking at it from the work or chore aspect, he won't cross that line. In this case, it has absolutely nothing to do with you; he is just living in the moment.

The Thrill of the Chase

Now, this is a good one, because it applies to both sexes. Again, we go back to the familiar game of cat and mouse. While some men and women pursue a potential mate, some pursue for sport. They want to know just how many numbers they can rack up. If more happens, especially in the sheets, it happens. But if not, they will generally move on to the next hunt. These types usually frequent clubs, bars, restaurants, etc. They are on dating apps. They try to have a prominent social media following. Their reputation and success of their chase depend on the persona they can create through these outlets. But again, once put on the spot, they will find a way not to be serious, and in some cases, admit that it was all in fun.

It's A Season

This is a funny one because I hear people say this all the time. They describe their friends as going through a season of random dating and frequently promiscuousness. The ironic thing about this one is that they often describe themselves in the present or describe themselves in the past. During this season, a lot of hearts are broken, as well as a lot of trusts. During this season, the person does not care who is hurt in the fray, as long as they get what they want in the end. The irony in this is that once this person comes out of that season, they are usually attracted to someone that is the same as they used to be, and it is often disastrous for both. Honestly, I think we have all been there, whether dating, sex, hobbies, self-exploration, or many other things. It's part of life. We as humans tend to take on a wave and ride it until we are done, and then it is on to the next. If you happen to stumble upon one in his/her season, tread lightly not to be hurt.

You Are Not Mama

That first sentence comes off a little weird, I know. But at the heart of it is the truth. Most men want someone that closely resembles traits found in their mother. They will seek that out diligently, and that is usually who they end up with long-term. And if a woman does not compare at least a little bit to mom, she is out the door. That is not to say that he won't still seduce you in the sheets; know he will not keep you unless there is a dramatic change in how you operate, aka being more like her. And if there isn't said change, buckle up for the ride. It could be a little bumpy before you get off. A telltale sign would be whether you are ever introduced to his mother or not. Hell, for that matter, aunts, female cousins, grandmother, etc. All these women have had a crucial role in raising him, and they will be able to discern whether you are the one for him or not.

After all, he's spent just about every single day with his mother, and he has seen everything she does during that time. So, if one person has the biggest impression on him and is what he will seek, it is her. And if you aren't, he likely won't even bother taking you her way.

Mothers also tend to have no filter, especially when it comes to their children's best interests. They will give him the complete, unadulterated truth, whether he wants to hear it or not. And usually, what she says is gospel. There is no other way around it. Even in death, he still lives by a lot of the principles she instilled in him. Does this make him a "mama's boy"? No, but like most people, she holds a special place in his heart and her word is her bond. If you've been kicking it for a while or dating, and you've yet to meet mom, introduce the idea to him. And if he has an excuse as to why he can't make that happen, take that sign and proceed accordingly.

Classism and Cliques

I think we have all been guilty of this at some point, whether it pertained to a relationship or just in life in general. We all have friends and associates based on things we have in common, kinships, attitudes, and even goals. These circles tend to be strong, and it can be hard, if not impossible, to let someone new in. This is where you come in. We've already established that the sexual relationship is there, and you guys enjoy that aspect of it. But unless your wants, needs, attitude, and goals match his (and likely those of his inner circle), you will never meet them. This can be especially true if they are married. Couples tend to be the most judgmental when setting the "standard" that the group will accept. The group may be very cordial and say/do all the right things while you're there, but best believe if they disapprove, they will let him know.

Personally, I used to be apprehensive when introducing someone new to my circle of friends for a few reasons.

First, my circle is permanent, so I looked at it from the perspective of potentially having this person in the circle forever. Second, what if I liked her and my friends didn't? I know that my happiness is more important, of course, but that tends to make for some pretty awkward gatherings and social events. Finally, what if they didn't like her and decided they wanted to point out every flaw to me? Now boundaries are being tested, and lines are being drawn. Being a non-confrontational person, I avoided it with many people because I knew how it would go. Most men do the same. Having said that, if he already knows how his friends are, you will be forever waiting on that invitation. That's not to say that it can't happen or that all friends are like this because opposites do attract, and I've seen it work a million times. But it can be uphill for a while, or at least until the friends warm up. I would suggest a very casual meet and greet, to introduce yourself to them. Depending on his response, it will tell you what you need to know about where you stand.

You Are Too Strong.

This one can be tough for some men because we are taught to be providers and protectors at a young age. It is an alpha mentality. That doesn't mean that we want to rule with an iron fist; we want to feel essential. Being too strong, whether in public, private, or even in the bed, can be a red flag to many men.

Conversely, some men do like aggressive women in the bedroom but prefer to be more subdued elsewhere. As an entrepreneur and someone with a mind for business, I like an assertive woman when it comes to certain things. By that same token, I can see how some men would be turned off. We are all different; what works for you may not work for me. This is where gender roles take effect. While I have no problem with it, some men believe a woman should know her place and be submissive in all things. So, when he encounters someone who is the opposite of these things, he doesn't know how to accept her and pursue it elsewhere. While it is natural to get angry or offended at his choice at first glance, we must remember that we all have "types," and we all have a mental list of things that we want. Some may be looked at as outdated, and some would be looked at as too progressive. But as they say, the heart wants what the heart wants. And more often than not, the heart will not stop until it gets what it wants.

The Feeling is Mutual

As much as we say this about men, have we ever considered that women might feel the same way about us as we think about them? The fun, the thrill of the chase, the season, and you may not be the daddy. The roles can be quickly reversed just like that. Having said all of that, I have found that women tend to be quite different in their approach as men. Most men will not show their hand or let their intentions be known until backed into a corner and forced to deal with the situation; women will often say what is on their minds. Whether it be friendship, dating to be dating, strictly sex, dating with a purpose, or even to get their feet wet again, they will put you on game off the top. And honestly, while it is a plus to know where you stand with a woman, it can also be intimidating. I say the intimidation factor arises because maybe he has been through all the steps and he's ready to date with a purpose and settle down. Hearing a woman say something that doesn't align with where he currently is can be a lot.

I prefer a woman to take control and tell me exactly what she wants, and I can move accordingly. So, if a man or woman tells you exactly what they want from you, believe them. This also goes along with timing. As I mentioned before, the timing may be off between the two parties. If they are on opposite ends of the spectrum, them trying to be together will be disastrous. Now, it may make for some great sex, but at the end of the day, it's still empty, with one expecting more out of the other while the other refuses to deliver. If it's not time, it's not time. Maybe the moon and stars will line up for you two, and perhaps it won't. But take that time to work on yourself and get better for when it does, whether it's with that person or someone else.

Trauma

This is a challenging subject, one that people don't wish to discuss. But it is just as natural as all the others I have described. There is a saying that hurt people hurt people. I used to wonder exactly what that meant. Until I was hurt by someone that had been damaged, it was an endless cycle until I was finally able to break it. I believe in spirits, both good and bad, and that they exist in all of us. The longer we are around a person, the more opportunity their energy has to latch on and take hold. I was in that situation. When it was good, it was great; but when it was terrible, it was awful. But I tried my best to stay in there, and in turn, I started to become the person I so desperately wanted to leave. So, when my next relationship came along, it wasn't good. I ended up in therapy because of it, but I knew that decision would be the best thing for me if I were ever to have any healthy, meaningful relationship in the future. This person will often take you out but degrade you so severely that you wish you stayed home. Fortunately, with a bit of help and a lot of willpower, this can be overcome. The signs will always be there, but it is up to you to be wary of them.

Commitment Issues

This is probably the most prevalent and common reason you will get only a tiny slice of the proverbial pie. Remember, sex and sleeping together are different entities. For example, a little sleepover might seem harmless and sweet to you, but it is one step closer to being a couple to a guy. This may sound far-fetched, and I get that. But it is true. You are already having sex, so how could sleeping together be a game-changing event? Think about it this way: just the act of waking up next to you and possibly having breakfast together signifies to him that you two are now an item. In his mind, everything has changed, and not necessarily for the best. The morning also means intertwined bodies, morning breath, no makeup, bedhead, and the dreaded pillow talk. He may not be ready for that kind of closeness yet. It may not be the most mature approach but taking off is his way of slowing things down only slightly; it is his correction maneuver. There may still be relationship potential; it's just too soon to tell.

Give him a little more time to sort things out in his head. Generally, it takes men longer to be comfortable with intimacy. Now, if he still wants to cut the night short after a few months, I think that is a clear sign. Now comes the sit-down with the tough questions. Ask him, in a non-accusatory way, why he won't spend the night. After he gives his reason (which could range from him having to get up and go to work or even tell you the truth that he doesn't want to), tell him how you feel. At this point, you can issue an ultimatum, but be careful. Depending on many factors, this could hurt or harm whatever it is that you have going on. Hopefully, he cares enough about keeping you in his life that he'll get past his sleepover aversion.

Top of Form

Though I have given all of these reasons why he can lay with you but not stay with you, I don't want you to be discouraged. Instead, embrace who you are, love who you are, respect who you are. Take the time out to figure out what you want to do; learn your passion. You may want to read more, go back to school, become a writer, take golf or tennis lessons, go skydiving, etc. Whatever it is, devote your time and attention to it and be the best you can be. Trust me; I know all too well about it. I am 38 years old, and I realized my true passion when I was 34. It can take some time, but continue to try new things or even rediscover the old until you get it. Enjoy the journey and every stage it gives you. There is a lesson behind them all.

Bless up.

Contributing Author
A.D. Roberts

A.D. Roberts is a successful author, success coach, and business developer, having started and grown several business concerns in real estate investment, finance, consulting film making, and network marketing. Over the years, his true passion has been empowering and inspiring people through motivational workshops, wellness retreats, and seminars highlighting the power of using hypnosis to improve one's life significantly. His story is a fantastic journey from having it all, losing everything, and bouncing back better than before! A.D. will be the first to tell you to *"keep watching because the journey is far from over."*

He is the founder of **Brilliant Living, Inc. (B.L.)**, a mind, body, and spirit wellness institute, **BrilliantFilmz**, a film company that has produced shows for the **Word Network** and **The Fortune Switch Show** that A.D. personally hosts. Most recently, he began his latest endeavor, InnerZenNow.com, the home for powerful self-hypnosis and guided meditation recordings. A.D. published **"Our Spirits Renewed,"** his first book, several years ago and is preparing to release his 2nd and 3rd books this coming year. He is also the producer of **The You 2.0 Series: From Serendipity to Synchronicity**, a major self-empowerment and reinvention course featured on **Udemy**. Mr. Roberts' personal objective is to build a community of people worldwide through **Brilliant Living** and **Inner Zen Now**, empowering the greatness of people's lives- helping them to manifest the passions of their hearts.

For more information and booking, visit:

www.ADRobertsNow.com

CHAPTER SIX

I Can't Compete with Ghosts

With
A. D. Roberts

The beauty and excitement of a new relationship are incredible. Everything starts so wonderfully, with happiness all around. We can see and feel the "possibilities" of how great our lives will be together. Our days are filled with dates, fun, and excitement. We can't wait to be around our new love. They make us feel alive again and filled with hope that finally, we have found "The One." We no longer have to go on dates with strangers, interviewing possible candidates for that special place in our hearts. We are "stick a fork in us" done. Why not? We deserve to be happy. It feels good to love and be loved in return. We can wrap ourselves up in this love like a warm blanket and lay around in it all day…until it happens.

We are happy with life until our new love does something, which triggers a slight fear in us. It could be something as simple as the wrong choice of words. It could be a small behavioral thing that makes us sit up and start to take note. "This looks familiar." "I have been here before." It might not even be something that our sweetheart does. It could be a conversation with a friend or a family member that triggers concern. And let's not forget social media. We could be casually scrolling on our favorite platform and come across a post that makes us begin to question a few things about our newfound love. Instead of focusing on that which is present and very real, we sacrifice the magic of "now" for the illusions that dance ever so quietly in our minds.

You see, many of us carry with us the pain, heartache, and disappointment of the past. At any given time, for any little reason, we can be triggered and brought out of our happy, blissful place into the drudgery of what happened a long time ago. These feelings stir the darkest of fears in us and, like poison, begin to eat away at the beautiful possibilities of our new relationship. Our old fears foster new fears that we project onto our present situation and taint it in a significant way. We start to look at our new love differently–our focus shifts from being free-heartedly in love to being guarded and watchful. We go from being a loving dreamer to being a taskmaster of never-ending queries, doubt, and anxiety. This mindset can only create mistrust and deliberate distancing for the "protection" of our hearts. At least that's what we tell ourselves. We tell ourselves that it's for the best that we remain cautious instead of saying "to hell with fear" and throwing caution to the wind to be madly in love.

To make these matters worse, we sometimes have broken and unhealthy people in our space, and they may not always want us to be happy while they aren't happy. As the old saying goes, "misery loves company." Our friends and family often, under the guise of "looking out for us," offer a never-ending supply of advice and opinion to fuel our love life's concerns. They constantly share their personal life experiences without any sense of objectivity or care that we may be preparing to miss out on the love that's truly meant for us. We have to remind ourselves that we are not them and they are not us. Our lives are our lives, and they are different. They indeed may love us and have the best of intentions sometimes, but never should we sacrifice the power of love's possibility for the cold empty embrace of fear - especially fear handed to us by the misery of someone else's misfortune. All of this robs us of how amazing our new love can be.

Unfortunately, many of us walk around carrying the faint shadowy trace of relationships that have gone on. We often wear them like badges on our chest or nooses around our neck, constantly sharing those experiences with new people that come into our lives. Sometimes we even measure our present moment situation by those *ghosts* of the past, whether they are our personal ghosts or ghosts shared with us viscerally from another.

What we need to understand is that those ghosts are ghosts for a reason. They are a part of our past, and that is where they should remain. When we hold on to the past by reliving it or playing those mental movies repeatedly, we perpetuate that old season's spirit in our lives. It locks us into a singular vibrational frequency, causing us to experience cyclical patterns of living. We get the same ole same ole. Also, we get the same old thing because many of us tend to "impress" upon others our fears, doubts, and trepidations.

Our new love cannot and should not be forced to wrestle with our ghosts of the past. It is sad enough that we are still embracing them, let alone imposing them on someone else. So, here are a few *ghostly* questions you should be asking yourself right now. Are you in a position to be dating in the first place? Do you have the right mindset to embrace the beautiful possibilities of new love in your life? Have you healed from your past trauma and pain? Are you looking for someone to help you get over your last relationship? Are you healthy enough to receive a healthy man or woman in your life? Do you have a good (not perfect) example of a loving, fulfilling relationship? Do you understand that no one is perfect, but they can be perfect for you?

Your answers to the questions above are vital to your well-being and the success of any new relationship you are considering. So, if you will, let's take a moment and examine just a few of these questions in your own experience.

Are you in a position to be dating in the first place?

This is simply fundamental. You have to be in a position mentally, emotionally, and spiritually that is healthy in order to engage someone in a new relationship.

Many of us wrestle with the voices of the past, and those voices constantly whisper to us, dictating our actions from day to day. It can be the voice of a family member that is rumbling around in our heads. It could also be the voice of a relationship long gone.

Nevertheless, we must be able to recognize the source of our decision-making process. Who is talking inside of our head? Ultimately, we have to ask ourselves, is this voice healthy? To determine if it is, we look to see *if that voice aligns with the things that our heart wants to experience*. Suppose our thoughts and our desires are not in alignment. In that case, vibrationally, we create this interference pattern that sometimes derails the possibility of having a healthy connection with someone who deserves one. Alignment is the key to so many things in our lives. This is most often where we make our biggest mistakes. We speak that we want to experience an excellent relationship with someone and that we want to be happy. However, the ghosts of our past interrupt those moments and begin to dictate something different. Because those dictates are so foreign, we seldom experience the true beauty of what we're looking for in a relationship or anything else for that matter. For us to attract anything into our space- our thoughts, our words, and our actions must be in alignment with one another. This will help put us in a position to be ready to date.

Do you have the right mindset to embrace the beautiful possibilities of new love in your life?

Your mindset has to be galvanized in the positive. Your thoughts have to arise from the healthy place, and that is whole. Broken people with broken hearts cannot create healthy holistic relationships. Quite often, what we are doing as broken people, we are looking for people to rescue us from the damage that we have allowed life to wreak upon us. This damage can come from a host of things: failed relationships, disappointments, our parents, financial setbacks, a place of living your compromise and not your life.

To increase the likelihood of having an excellent relationship, having a positive and hopeful mindset means a great deal. For the best outcome, we have to be anchored in that which *can be* beautifully possible. I have always said that our focus brings about our reality. What we focus on most we attract into our space. It must manifest itself in our lives. Having a positive mental attitude will allow you to focus on the positive things. If you believe that you can have a great connection with someone, then the likelihood of having that connection is possible. However, if you're constantly questioning and doubting the beauty of that connection, the probability of that connection being a good one is slim to none. Having the right mental attitude as you approach any situation in any relationship is vital to its' success. To help eliminate the ghosts that may get in your way, I recommend that you write down affirmative statements as it pertains to exactly what you want to experience. "I am happy and healthy, and my heart is ready for a healthy relationship." "I love myself, and I am ready to be loved."

"Love flows to me easily and effortlessly because my heart is open." Statements like these, repeated daily, will foster the proper mental space for you to vibrate at the right frequency to attract into your life that which you wish to experience. You see, for everything that you want to experience, you must be the thing first. You must be a vibrational match for that thing. Using daily affirmations will slowly saturate your subconscious mind, and those words will become a part of who you see yourself as. As your mind begins to shift to this new place, you will then begin to attract new experiences into your space. This is the power of a positive mental attitude.

Have you healed from your past trauma and pain?

Healing before attempting to date is wise and mature. Recovering before you date says that you are now ready to engage in something fresh and new. You would never put on a beautiful new white shirt while you are still bleeding from a terrible cut, would you? When you have given yourself time to heal from a previous relationship that had you broken and sad, you clear yourself of the old vibrational frequencies. Freeing yourself from the old opens the pathway for new vibrations. These new vibrations create new possibilities. Going into a new relationship and not being healed will only drag those old experiences, old habits, old thoughts, and old ghosts into the new one. You are not only doing yourself a disservice, but you are doing a significant detriment to the beautiful possibilities of your new relationship.

Let's face it; healing is everything. It would help if you gave yourself time to recover from a season that broke you.

Unfortunately, in addition to broken relationships, many women suffer from daddy issues that have never been addressed, let alone resolved. Anything in your life that is unresolved, and you try to start something new, bring that old season into the new season. Doing this brings about stress and anxiety. I know that it's hard, but you have to do the work. You have to face your demons head-on. If you don't do the work, you're going to constantly get the same results over and over and over again. You have to give yourself a fair chance at happiness. It's like taking an entire day preparing a wonderful meal to serve it on some old dirty dishes. It just doesn't make sense. If you won't do that with your food, why would you even consider doing that with your life? Get counseling. Seek therapy that is objective. Talk to a professional or a person that doesn't know you personally. You deserve something amazing, and healing yourself is just the beginning you need.

Are you looking for someone to help you get over your last relationship?

Many times, people look for distractions from the mundane reality of their lives. There are times when people aren't looking for a relationship. They are looking for someone to help them forget about the past pains enough to silence the feeling of that hurt. So, are you looking for someone to help you get over your last situation? Doing so is one of the most selfish acts you can perform. If this is what you're doing, it's not going to work for very long. This will only end in heartache and brokenness for someone. No one deserves to be the *rebound* person. You wouldn't want it done to you. Please don't do it to anyone else. Spend the time you need alone to heal and prepare yourself for something real. Unfortunately, most people want a shortcut to happiness. There are no shortcuts, and you will soon learn that *happiness is the way* to happiness (that's another discussion altogether). You will never arrive at happiness by taking a deceitful route or looking for it outside of yourself. This is why many people have become *serial daters.* That type of happiness is cheap and very short-lived. In the long run, you will end up paying the hefty price of loneliness.

Open your heart first. You have to be honest with yourself about where you are, where you've been, and where you would like to be. Then and only then will you be able to attract and maintain something healthy and whole. Someone once shared a statement with me that said, "hurt people hurt people." It was short, sweet, and to the point. Over my life, I have discovered this simple statement to be there true. If you have hurt within you, you will eventually share that hurt with someone else by breaking them, even if it isn't intentional. Using someone new to get over your old situation can be convoluted and self-defeating. This is a shortcut that often takes you down a path you genuinely don't want to venture.

Do you have a good (not perfect) example of a loving, fulfilling relationship? Do you understand that no one is perfect, but they can be perfect for you?

Most of our lives' successes come to us because we have had exposure to a pretty good example of what that particular success looks like. It gives us a visible goal, something to strive for. These examples of success can be inspiring and motivating. They also can sometimes help us map out a path to get there. This goes for relationships too. Have you ever witnessed a healthy relationship? We must have models in our lives of that which we wish to experience. I remember asking a couple what the secret to their 20 years of a happy marriage was, and their response was simple, *"we love each other the same way, at the same time."* Having this model has helped me tremendously over the years. Models like these become goals or targets for us to hit. The key is that they must be healthy and holistic and not superficial.

I often see people use the #relationshipgoals and what they're talking about as goals are primarily material–going on exotic trips to luxurious locations and purchasing big beautiful houses and expensive cars. These are nice things, but picture-perfect relationships are displayed wonderfully on social media. Should they be relationship goals? There are no perfect relationships, but there are those who strive for good, honest and healthy. Somewhere in your space, seek to connect with couples that are happy together. Look for their counsel. Not always will their counsel be rooted in words but found in the wonderful example of their day-to-day lives with one another. One of the things that I found from healthy relationships is that they understood going in that no one is perfect, but their partner can be perfect for them. Looking at someone's imperfections and finding perfection is beautiful.

Set yourself up for success and not failure by excepting your shortcomings and being honest about them. You don't have to be perfect to be loved, and you should never look for someone that is perfect to love. We all want love. We need it. If you say you don't, then you're lying to yourself. None of us are perfect, and many times we find it hard to see the beauty in ourselves. In this, you must learn to love yourself as you are, not your representative, not the illusions that you portray to the world. Learn to trust that with pure intentions and a clear heart, the love that you are looking for will present itself to you.

It's time to clean out your closet and get rid of the old garments of seasons that have passed. Move beyond the ghosts of relationships that failed and push past pain that has left you broken. You deserve something fresh a new, and beautiful. You deserve a new wardrobe, one that fits your new season, your new life, your new love. Your new love doesn't need to wrestle with the ghosts of your past any longer, and neither do you.

Contributing Author
David C. Dove I

What is it that inspires and fuels you? For the entrepreneur, director of music & youth leader David C. Dove, it's the opportunities given to reach a generation that others could not. As a black man growing daily, learning from every experience afforded to him, it's always been his goal to seize the moment. Taking in everything he possibly can to make himself better and others' lives that he may encounter.

Growing up, David has always been bold and outgoing. At the age of 5, he was already in front of large audiences bringing hope, joy, and happiness into their lives through music. Having no idea at that age how powerful his gift would become, David was drawn to it even more and has since then grown to higher heights and blessed to continue that path. While some people may not figure out until later in life what their passion is, for over 22 years,

David has been fortunate to know and embrace it and operate in it. Having his first professional music teaching job while in 12th grade was exciting enough, but having traveled and worked with artists such as Jay Z, Lauryn Hill, Savion Glover, The Sister Act II tour, Kirk Franklin, Shirley Caesar, John P Kee, and Hezekiah Walker to name a few were some of David's most incredible memories.

As exciting as those experiences were, nothing made David prouder than becoming the Shed Academy Performing Arts Youth Program's Founder to expose this generation to unique gifts and talents that he calls family and friends. His purpose is to be a risk-taker and bridge a gap between the now and next generation by mentoring, sharing, and showing love. David has many accomplishments, but the greatest of them was finding his wife Shayla Dove and having six wonderful children with her. Denae, David II, Caleb, Brent, Cameron, and Liam. Together they are #DoveDynasty and

#DemDoveBoysandaSis. David continues to live on purpose, embracing the process and trusting God through it all.

CHAPTER SEVEN

I Married Her Because I Could Not Trust You

With
David C. Dove I

Now before you look at those nine words and get the wrong idea, give me just a few moments of your time and let me explain.

Relationships are formed every day, whether as children growing up in our neighborhoods or schools, as a youth on your first few summer or part-time jobs, or as young adults entering college or the work field. Those are the first beginning moments of interaction outside of our homes and families. Those are the moments when you must use your instincts, intuition, and survival skills to see what's good or bad for you, to see what's right or wrong. I think we can all agree that everything we've experienced in our youth hasn't always been good or right for us. Although it might have been enjoyable at times but not necessarily the best for us, we didn't think much about it because we were young. We were living life, constantly feeling as if we had time and taking chances.

Remember growing up as kids and calling someone in school your best friend? Our parents would say they're not your best friend. They're your classmate. Immediately we would get a little offended. Like they are my best friend but not realizing that the reason our parents told us that was because they understood that those kinds of relationships take time, experience, and chemistry to build. Being that young, you would have a different best friend every other day. Very few of us are best friends or even close friends with your childhood buddies now, and to be honest with you, there's nothing strange about that at all. People grow, change and move on and as a result, you learn that that's life, and sometimes, you're not always the right fit for one another. Nothing wrong with that, is it? No, of course not. Life brings about change daily, and some of us have learned very early in life how to adjust and move on. As adults, we tend to forget about those life lessons and become more sensitive or offended when these things begin to happen.

When the relationship begins to change or not quite play out as you planned, it makes you feel away. Sure, when you're the one deciding to end a relationship and move on, you're doing what's best for you, protecting yourself and as you should. The issue occurs when you're not in the driver's seat, and now a decision is being made that you don't like, want, agree with, or have any control over the matter, but that person is protecting themselves. Sometimes we forget that we have a right to protect ourselves first. Some may feel that's a selfish attitude to have, and I say if there's ever a time to be selfish, it should be protecting what you value. Your heart and your time fall in that category of things to appreciate. Those are things we cherish. Our time, well, we already know we can't get that back once it's gone and heartbreak; who wants to go through that if we can avoid it, right?

Looking after us and not allowing anyone to take that from us is not only unselfish but wise and encouraged. Now don't get me wrong, giving access to our heart and most delicate spaces will happen when in a relationship, but why not choose who you give that access? Shouldn't we be able to choose who we share that space with? Yes. It's essential, and that kind of access shouldn't be granted until a person has proven they're ready, willing, and able to handle that role and position in your life. That was why our parents told us what they did when speaking about the childhood best friend. Ready, willing, and able, meaning they're at a place in life where they're tired of the game playing, looking forward to a more serious involvement, and mature enough for what comes with it. Willing to take the necessary steps to show you how committed they are to making this next chapter in life a priority without any excuses and handling the pressures and ups and downs that may come along the way.

I know what you're thinking; how is it that you know who that person is or when that time is? Listen, everyone knows how they would like to feel when being in a relationship and even more in marriage. You may have even pictured it and played it over and over in your mind more times than you can count.

Maybe you don't have every detail mapped out, but in general, you have imagined some form of what you think it would and should be and what you would like it to feel like. You've already given it much thought, and this often happens long before you find Mr. or Mrs. Right. That was the beginning of knowing what you were looking for. I know it's been said that men aren't as into marriage or committed relationships as women until they are. Yes, ladies, men think about marriage and long-term commitment, just not with every woman we come in contact with. I'm not sure who put that out there that men don't want to be married and happy just like you ladies, but somehow, it's been put out there. I often have this conversation with my wife of 18 years that men and women are very much alike. We both want love. We both want quality time. We both want someone we can share and build with. We both want happiness. We both want affection.

We both want to be the first thing you think of in the morning and the last thing you think of at night. We both have desires and pleasures we'd like fulfilled. We both love to have every need met. We both have insecurities and things we're working on daily to better ourselves. We both get jealous at times. We both want to feel that no one can ever take our place, be in the same position or on the same level as us when it comes to the relationship. Sure, we may express it differently, but we're thinking the same. The only difference between us is that men tend not to communicate this early or show our heart as easy. We're not as quick to open up and share until we feel like we can trust you. So, as a way of protection and being cautious, we won't allow anyone into that space or have that kind of access. You don't give someone that kind of access until you feel you can trust them with it. Sure, you may think someone is cute or beautiful; maybe they have a relaxed vibe and presence about them, perhaps they seem as if they have it all together, but they still don't gain access until you can trust them. Trust is tricky. It isn't earned overnight. It can't be built without going through the good and bad processes in life or the highs and lows, but trust must be tested and tried on so many levels.

It's the kind of thing that you can't just point out. I believe you only have two natural ways of knowing it, 1. what your gut tells you and 2. the track record of an individual. Whichever works for you or happens first, the bottom line is both require time. This may be a bit more difficult these days with everything being so misleading and most often looking like a big front. If you look even on social media and television, it's tough to tell the real from the fake. Everything appears to be so programmed and produced. It's difficult to tell what's true or false.

Here's the thing, trust can't be manipulated by how good you look or cook, how sweet your voice sounds, the clothes you wear, the car you drive, not even with the promises you make, the things you may buy and most definitely not even with sex; but it has to be earned. Those things are excellent and can even make you feel good for a moment, but if you think that's the thing that will make someone commit, I'm sorry to say it's not. There must be action behind those promises. Just as women should expect from men, trust and believe a man is not committing until then. The trust has to be there and has to be earned.

I hear a lot of women say that men are visual, and you're right. We are, but we're so much more than visual. We're not only attracted to what we see, but we're also attracted to what we feel and what we think about you. When you put the two together, it's a good problem for us to have. Men are thinkers and planners. We have thoughts and plans as to how we see the future of our relationship. We're goal-driven, and although we may still strive for things to come to fruition, the goals are there. We're fathers and husbands, and just as you ladies have thoughts about finding that perfect love and having children, so have we. We're businessmen, and like every good business, we know that its success is built with a great team and partnership.

Who better to do that with than a person we can trust. Who better to allow in your inner circle. A person who wants you to win just as much as you, a person who sees your weaknesses and flaws and rather than remind you of it and bring you down, find ways to lift you because the bigger picture is when one of us wins, we all win. Marriage and relationships are all about trust. The more you trust one another, the stronger the bond. The more you trust one another, the more confident you feel leaning and depending on each other. When you trust someone, you rarely question or second guess their input, but you look forward to their input, thoughts, and opinions. This doesn't take anything away from being your own individual or having your own identity, but when you trust someone and see and feel their intentions, you're more open to what they add to you. Trust is the doorway to some of the most intimate moments in a relationship. When the trust is there, things are magical. Even on difficult days, trust helps you get through it. Without it, it's impossible to have anything solid. There's no true love without trust.

Many women may have felt over the years that the reason a relationship didn't work out was that they did something wrong, or that the man was playing games, and it's entirely possible that you did, or he was, but in many cases, it may not have been either. A man will only settle and marry someone he feels will add to him being a better man. Not that you're not a good woman, ladies but hear me out. It takes a specific type of woman to add value to your life in a way that you didn't even know that she did until it was done. Meaning she knows how to encourage you without you showing signs of even needing encouragement. When you did without her asking what's wrong, she used her intuition, began to make changes, started thinking of solutions, and made things happen to help release loads of stress, worries, and frustrations. She knows how to stay on your case without it feeling like nagging. She knows how to love you and challenge you to push yourself even harder and further and have you feeling good about it. Yep, that part. The only woman that can do those things is a woman that a man trusts.

A man is not above putting in the work, and if you've been brought up in my day, you had a father or grandfather that would not allow you as a man to not put in the work for who you loved. Even on the days that it may seem complex or challenging, you're already conditioned to the grind and do what it takes to make it work.

When we trust a woman with our heart, we're all in. When we trust you, we change all of our rules. When we trust you, all the things we said we would never do go out the window. When we trust you, all of our boys and close family know that we're in a different place in life. A place that no other woman was able to get us to. When we trust you, we're not ashamed of you, not embarrassed to share you with the rest of our world. There's a certain level of comfort and security for us as men knowing that there's someone in our life that we can be our total complete self with. When we trust you, we're willing to share our deepest thoughts and darkest secrets. When we trust you, we share our biggest dreams and scariest nightmares. That's the woman we look forward to coming home to, a woman we want to spend time with daily. Ask yourself when the last time a man shared their biggest dreams and goals or their most frightening nightmares was? If all you know about him is, he likes you in heels, he wants your hair a certain way, he likes seafood, and to grill, he enjoys sports and reading. That's nice, but that's so surface. He doesn't trust you enough to even share more with you than the things everyone else could figure out just from paying attention.

Some of you have been dating for years and found yourself repeating cycles, and then one day, the relationship went left. The same guy you were with for years that never proposed or talked about taking things to the next level has all of a sudden gotten married and moved on. I know your initial reaction is, The Nerve of Him!! I've been here all these years, and he's going to marry her. Maybe you even questioned yourself, thinking you did something wrong, saying it's your fault. It's at that moment when the guy would say one of the most famous lines ever created, "It's not you, but it's me," but in this case, it's so true. Ladies, it's nothing you could have done to change his mind.

What he's saying is, I Married Her Because I Couldn't Trust You. He couldn't trust that you would be the woman he needed in his life. He couldn't trust you to be the woman he would want to build a future with. The woman he would like to start a family with. He couldn't trust you to share his plans, hopes, and dreams. He couldn't trust you to be that strength and motivation that he would need. He couldn't trust you to be your own woman, move to your beat, and not get caught up with everyone else. He couldn't trust you to hang in there if times got bad and things got rough. He couldn't trust you to make sacrifices and think about the bigger picture. He couldn't trust you to stop being in competition with all your girls and comparing the relationship to them. He couldn't trust you to be strong and confident, even if it meant disagreeing with loved ones. He couldn't trust you because maybe you got caught up with the surface things. Perhaps you never paid attention to him and his thoughts. Perhaps you just weren't the right fit, and he finally accepted it. Maybe you didn't give the proper introduction for him to know all of who you were, so he never found a safe space in opening up to you. Maybe you were so happy with just being in a relationship and kept things on a level that didn't appear attractive or promising.

Maybe you never even realized he wanted more. Perhaps you never acknowledged the signs and the things that were said that you might have ignored. Maybe you thought you were best friends and would live happily ever after when in reality, you were just classmates.

Now a decision has been made for you that you have no say or control over the matter. Sure, there's hurt that comes from the thought of all the time that was wasted and lost, but, in all fairness, it wasn't meant to be. He decided to protect himself, to be selfish, and decide before even more time was wasted. The truth is it sounds so cold and insensitive. In this case, it's the man moving on and making a choice for himself. But how many times has a woman moved on because she couldn't trust that the man would step up and be what she needed? No harm, no foul. Life changes daily, and the day we acknowledge that the better off we'll all be.

You can't force love; you can't force trust, and you can't force a relationship. If it's meant to be, it will be. But if it's not, it won't. No matter how hard you try to fight for it. No matter how long you try to hold on, eventually, the grip gets looser. The truth is, just as we know, there's nothing there you know as well. Just as we feel that something is off, and the connection is just not flowing, you feel it as well. The best thing to do is to let go and find the right match. There's someone out there for you. You're strong;

you're smart, you're attractive, you're confident, you're all those beautiful things. You are a powerful woman! And you should be free and find who's right for you rather than have regrets years later. More importantly, it's better to find someone you can trust and can trust you. After all, I Married Her Because I Could Not Trust You!!!

Contributing Author
C.J. Randolph

Are you ignoring understanding or learning from it? Put that understanding into action, and now you have wisdom. CJ Randolph has taken his and others' life experiences and turned that wisdom into inspiration. His idea is to see the beauty of perspective no matter if it different then his own. In seeing other's views, you can form a better understanding of a situation and move forward. Dealing with his battles in life, he gained wisdom that allowed him to decide to be better. Those decisions meant he had to reflect on oneself action and walk down the difficult road of healing…. himself. Now on the other side, he considers himself a messenger of the gospel, aka the good news. The message of love, hope, faith, and most of all, peace.

He is a 7th grade Science teacher and 8th-grade football, basketball, and track coach. He has been in education for ten years and loves working and spreading the message to his students that they have the ability to be excellent in their future. With hard work and consistency, you can have a great life. Being honest and authentic is something he prides himself on with whoever he is talking with. He understands the balance of the audience he is talking to and how to deliver the information they can digest to gain nutrition.

Stop living your life in the state of gray…aka average. You were created to do great things; it's in your DNA! Live your life in full vibrance and show the light that has always been within you. As Marianne Williamson says in "Our Deepest Fear," <u>And as we let our own light shine, we unconsciously give other people permission to do the same</u>. So, shine on – Selah

CHAPTER EIGHT

Your Children Are A Blessing, Just Not Mine

With
C. J. Randolph

Now let me start by saying that I believe all children are a blessing as for they are miracles. The Bible says, "Children are a heritage from the Lord, offspring a reward from the Lord." Psalms 127:3. I consider myself a man of scripture, but I have lived enough life to struggle to understand that verse fully. Why, you ask? I teach 7th-grade science and coach 8th-grade boys' football, basketball, and track…Nuff said!

As a teacher, we have "Meet the Teacher Night" each year, and this is where I tell the parents and students that this a collaboration of all of us to help make the student not just successful in class but also life. I teach life through a subject, and science is perfect for doing that. I let the parent (usually the mother) and the child understand that I know that this is your baby…but they are not mine. See, I like to establish that there is a relationship dynamic that has three parties involved. I set the precedence of who I am and who I will be in my students' and parents' lives. I give them an expectation that I will work to live up to, and in return, I have an expectation that they are to live up to. Nothing too strenuous, just that if they step outside of that in my classroom, here are the consequences. Through the year, the truth will let me see if what they were telling me about themselves. My dad has a quote I grew up hearing all the time. "Your actions speak so loud; I can't understand what you are saying." I have come up with something that speaks into action. "May my words be filled with action so that they no longer remain empty." The Bible says to stay away from those that speak empty words. I have heard so many times, "O my baby would never….", yes ma'am yo baby did."

Actions

Why am I talking about empty words and actions so much? Well, because it has everything to do with a relationship, especially involving kids. Many times, we have blinders on about our children. We view them as innocent little humans, especially mothers. In my experience and the experiences of many other men during our "barber shop" talks, it comes up that a woman's kids can make or break a relationship, or to put it better, how a woman handles her children can make or break a relationship.

Love, It's Not All the Same

For the most part, there is the love of a mother and the love of a father. They are different and expressed in different ways but very integral in the overall development of a child. That initial design has been broken for several reasons that we do not have to go into because many of us have lived them. There are gaps that mothers must fill that was not intended for them to fill. A mother's love is more nurturing as a father's love promotes inner growth and strength. Here is an example that repeats through the ages that show the difference. A child scrapes their knee, and that mother says, "Here, sit down, let me kiss it make it better." And the father says, "You're alright, throw some dirt on it and get back out there and play." Both are love, but there is a time and place for one to take precedence over the other; it is designed that way.

Intentions

The way you treat your child is significant to a man who wants to build with you. Now let me interject and clarify that this is strictly for those seeking a future with you. I believe you should be intentional with your intentions. First, you must know your preferences and then hold him to the standard of what he has said. The phases of a relationship should be to date, to court, and to marry. If you are not sure of his intentions, then there is no reason to introduce him to your child or children. Since the foundation is laid and the clarity has been clarified, let get down to the nitty-gritty.

Communication

Communication is key. Yes, we have heard this our whole life, but do we understand how powerful it is when done correctly. Communication is a two-way street, not just you talking and him listening, but you listening to his response and vice versa. It would be best if you were willing to ask the tough questions upfront, not to assume anything in a relationship. That is where we all can get caught up, giving someone an implicit expectation and then treating them like they are aware that they are not living up to it. Be transparent and open about what your intentions are. If he cannot understand that, then keep it moving. Do not waste your time. What you accept in the beginning is what he expects in the future. As it comes to your children, he should want to learn you as who you are, not necessarily a mother but as a partner. He does not need a mother, and if he does, then RUN RUN RUN!

Don't Be A Nagger!

Speaking of running, he may be the one that is doing the running, and that may be your fault. It is not necessarily something that you are doing but maybe something that you are not...disciplining your "little angels." As mentioned before, a father's love and a mother's love look and feels different, and that's ok. We humans always have the issue that we expect others to love, feel, react, and act like ourselves. So, when you do not see the beauty in his perspective, he can view it as judgmental, unattractive, or quintessentially nagging. PLEASE DONT BE A NAGGER! I get it; your babies will always be your babies, but they are not his babies. Yes, you think I know that, but sometimes amid progression towards marriage, you can lose hindsight in that. As he and they start to blend into a family, situations put you right back into reality. The quickest way for that to happen is when your child(ren) acts up, and you do not handle it in a way that makes you look like they disrespect you.

Attention

He is paying attention.... close attention. He is also wondering a lot, processing what he observes. He may let you know, or he may monitor and assess. That is why no matter which method he uses, both of you are communicating what is going on, with no judgment or nagging. Remember, men are logical. Not saying that he is not emotional, much like I am not saying that you aren't rational, but the foundation of our thoughts first stems from logic. Much like we display a different type of love, we also have a different kind of logic. So, when observing how you and your child(ren) interact, he is trying to figure out where he fits in. He is wondering, "I am going to have to be the discipliner?" "Should I just back up and let her handle this, or "if it gets out of hand, how do I proceed in letting the kids know this is not acceptable?" "How do I do that without making her feel a certain way?" He is processing a lot, and some men may be more vocal in their approach, and others may be able to tolerate it for a time. Still, there needs to be communication between both of you because he thinks of things he would do if you all continued to the path of marriage. It comes down to the famous song by Aretha Franklin R-E-S-P-E-C-T.

Respect

The Bible says for a husband to love his wife and for a wife to respect her husband. Respect is tremendous in the heart and mind of a man because that is the way we are wired. If you allow your child(ren) to disrespect you, then there will be issues in the future in his eyes. I repeat IN HIS EYES. No King wants his Queen to be disrespected, even if it is from the little prince or princess, especially if they are not his. You may not see it as disrespect, but he may. Can those issues be worked out? Of course, they can, but are you willing to listen to his concerns and balance incorporating his ideas with your children. I get it…that can be tough. Some of you ladies out there have been holding it down for the family for a long time all by yourself, but an honest talk can bring clarity on how to move forward together…or separate. In his mind, if they are disrespecting you, then they will disrespect him. Right now, you may be the leading authority in their life, so all respect flows from you with the help of a teacher, a coach, or mentor but should start and end with you. Being a teacher and coach, I see it all too often. They are on the phone with their mom and giving her an attitude that I have to put them in check. In my daddy/coaching voice, "I better not ever hear you talk to your momma like that again, do you understand me!" Every year, I have to have a sit-down conversation with some of them on respecting their mom. It is very, very rare I have to have that conversation with them about their dad. If it gets to a point with my students that I must call their parents, they always want me to reach their mother, not their father. There are times that even with talking with the mother, I have to call the father to get the behavior to change permanently. My kids act differently with me and their mom. They learned at a very young age what heartstrings they could pull with each of us.

Get in Where He Fits In…or Out

You must understand that he is looking to be a part of your life, including your children. He is looking at where to fit in and add value to your life, much like what you can do to add value. In that value, he wants to be himself. If you allow him to be his authentic self, it is easier to see if he is the one to stay around. It is better for him not to be his representative and who he is rather than deceive you. The truth is we all do it in some form or fashion. Put our best foot forward and hide our ugly truths. I hope you would rather know some of those nasty truths before introducing them to your children. The truth is he may not feel like he can be his authentic self around your children because of judgment or the balance of his spot in the relationship with them. He may not allow what your children do to you to be done to him or even to you in his presence. Yes, there is compromise and understanding, but you have to understand that some things just aren't going to fly around him. If you all can't agree to figure it out together, maybe together is not what you all should be. It will come up in the future, especially if you intend to be married and be a family. What he allows at the beginning is usually the expectation of what is allowed later. Being a teacher who has taught for over ten years, the advice given to a young teacher is, "Be mean at first and then be nice." Yes, I know it sounds horrible right, it is a running joke, but the idea is accurate.

Dealing with kids in the school environment, they will see your weakness and exploit it every time they get a chance. And yes, kids instantly give more respect to male teachers than they do their female teachers faster. I did not make that up, but I see it in the hallways every day. So, it is vital as a teacher if you do not establish strong classroom management, then chaos is just around the corner. So, it is essential as a mother that who you invite into their life is about to establish themselves in the relationship. You don't want your children to get used to the version of what you want him to be and then not be who he is in the future. That is a disservice to him, you, and your children. He does not want to start with a weak foundation, and neither should you.

Perspective

Now let me get real with you. Yes, your children are a blessing, and much like blessings, it is your responsibility to take care of those blessings. I repeat your responsibility, not his until he takes on that responsibility. And like blessings, we tend to think that others see our blessings the same way we do….and that can be so far from the truth.

Really what it comes down to is perspective. Men and women are different, and there is a beauty in that if we could see would understand a situation better, but we don't. Your children can be stopping something great because of the way you view them and view him. Are you looking for someone to take on a daddy role? Are you looking for someone to take care of you and your children financially? Are you looking at this man to be the knight in shining armor or, in be in a more blunt way, "Captain Save A Hoe?" Well, that last part may be a question he is asking himself, or at least others may be asking him. We don't want to be hurt, and there are always concerns with dealing with any relationships, especially with children involved. Remember, perspective matters, and seeing his side of it can help you see a bigger better picture. That picture may paint your children in a different light than you may not want to see. One of my favorite lyrics is valid in all of life...*Sometimes the truth hurts, but deception always kills. Love can blind us to reality, especially when that is the love for a child, but deception is a killer, especially when you do it to yourself.*

Recap

Woah, now I know that we have just covered a lot of information that may have been hard to reflect and understand but believe me, you can benefit much from it. Yes, your children are a blessing, but your actions with them prove that they can bless others. Love is many things and, in many forms, and find the incredible power behind that. Be intentional with your intentions, and don't be afraid to communicate that. Please don't be a nagger, and he is paying close attention to everything, especially how you respect him. Now that he can trust you, respect him, he is looking to fit in the puzzle of your life. His perspective can enlighten you to some things that you may not have noticed, so at least give it a thought. It may not be the same as yours, but that does not mean that it is wrong. It's just different. If you allow your children to disrespect him, the primary key is to let him leave respectfully. He wants to know that he matters in your life as your man, that he can trust you to be there when he needs you. He wants you to be there to pick him up if he was down, to help restore the king inside of him. Sometimes that focus can be placed within your children, and when it is, he may look elsewhere for that trust. There is a beautiful balance there, ladies…never forget that. It may take some time to find it, but when you find it, hold on to it, and you can have his heart, mind, and body.

Contributing Author
Jason Hendrickson

Jason Hendrickson epitomizes the moniker of a man of many talents, first gaining notoriety as a master percussionist for Bishop Hezekiah Walker and the Love Fellowship Crusade Choir. His musicality and adeptness led to additional touring opportunities with Lost Boyz/ Mr.Cheeks and Faith Evans, to name a few. As a songwriter, he has penned music for several of his projects and Grammy and Stellar Award-winning recording artist Marvin Sapp. Jason Hendrickson's music fulfills a mission to use everyday life experiences to encourage and uplift people to renew their hope in God. The Singles EP places some of Hendrickson's compositions together in a musical buffet for the listeners' delight, both loyal fans and new devotees alike.

Hendrickson was awarded an honorary Doctor of Sacred Music from ABG Seminary and is an in-demand speaker, life catalyst, and published author. He is a powerful preacher and teacher of the Gospel as well as a tastemaker and influencer. On the entrepreneurial side, he is the CEO of All Things Apparel, which features a robust clothing line and recently moved into culinary dessert creations and an extensive gourmet coffee line.

CHAPTER NINE

Your Spirituality Is M.I.A

With
Jason Hendrickson

One of the worst things that can happen to an individual is for you to meet someone stunning on the outside, but after one conversation, you discover that they are empty on the inside. Unfortunately, in this culture, we have people who have mastered the art of ostentation and would prefer to look at the part rather than to be the part. Looks can be highly deceitful and cause you to believe that you have ended up with what is your dream mate, and, in all actuality, you have ended up with an extreme nightmare. As of late, within the last year or so, we all have had to wear masks, but some people have had on a mask way before COVID-19, and I believe that this is the result of us not being comfortable with who we are.

Understanding the importance of spirituality becomes a red flag when looking to move forward in a relationship.

The ideal relationship is based on the things you have in common with the person you are in a relationship with. And you may ask, what role does spirituality play in all of this? Spirituality is based on the connection you have with God. The value of a relationship is based on how well you can connect on intellectualism levels, things that you do socially, financially, and of course, emotionally. To say that someone's spirituality is M.I.A. is saying that there is no connection, and this is a red flag for any relationship.

When this is discovered, it is not the end or the deal-breaker, but there must be immediate repair done if there is hope for the relationship to last. One of the things that will allow this breach to be repaired is the one that is missing the spirituality to be open to honest communication, and that is a problem for a lot of people. Most people only enjoy hearing what they want to hear and not what they need to hear. Knowing that the connection is broken and your partner being in the space where they can make such a solid statement to you is a beautiful foundational beginning for a healthy conversation. For anyone to feel this way and communicate these feelings is a blessing, although most people might be offended by this statement.

To identify and understand this statement, we must deal with what makes our connection or our spirituality between God and us strong, and that would be prayer. One of the things that makes it easy to have a healthy relationship between God and us is that the communication is conducted in a safe space. I can talk to him from a transparent perspective. I can also feel that he cares about what I'm saying; therefore, it makes me concerned about the health of our connection because the relationship has developed into a give-and-take concept. We have to think about why an individual's spirituality is Mia in a relationship, and we have to consider if we are the cause of it. Because again, if the communication between two people does not create a safe space for honesty, this will always be an issue.

This statement is powerful because it creates an opportunity for self-reflection and a transparent look into the relationship's health. Again, because we are talking about spirituality, I don't believe that we can talk about spirituality without dealing with the relationship that we have with God. From the beginning, God has gone out of his way to reassure us that the intent for his relationship or desire to be in a relationship with us was because of love. And when you look at the love of God, it is identifiable because of two words intent and extent. This is displayed to us in the book of John the 3rd chapter and the 16th verse, which says, "For God so love the world that he gave his only begotten son that whosoever believeth in him should not perish but have everlasting life." The intent was for

God to show the world just how much he loved us, and by giving his son, who was the only begotten son, was the extent he was willing to go to prove how much he loved us. Because of the intent and scope being so visible, it created and continues to create a certain comfort level that makes it easy to communicate with God. When there is a connection that has been broken in any relationship, someone inside of the relationship has to be able to detect the need to create a safe space so that the connection can be repaired. That can only happen where there is healthy communication between the two parties.

If you are going to be bold enough to make a statement like this, you must be prepared for the response, and you should be ready to provide a certain level of assistance in bringing this issue to a resolution. As you can see by the direction, I am taking regarding writing this chapter; this is a loaded statement. This can reveal so many different things about the individual making the statement and the individual the statement is being made about. We must be cautious when making a statement like this because it can become borderline judgmental and offensive if it is not resolved. This is one of those things where it matters not what you say but how you say it can make all the difference in the world.

When you look at the definition of spirituality, it is the quality of being concerned with the human spirit or soul instead of material or physical things. It also involves recognizing a feeling or sense of belief that something greater than me, something more to being human than sensory experience. The greater whole of which we are part is cosmic or divine in nature. An opening of the heart is an essential aspect of true spirituality. So, when you tell someone that their spirituality is missing, you tell them in so many words that they are selfish and care more about material and physical things than they do people. Depending on the culture of your relationship, this can be extremely helpful or very damaging. Let's explore the differences.

Let's say you are dating or married to someone insecure and overly emotional. This can be highly damaging because upon hearing a statement like this, the guards will automatically go up. On the contrary, if you are dating or married to a secure, analytical that loves to hear the truth about themselves to better themselves, this will be one of the most significant breakthroughs you will experience in the relationship. The insecure individual will take this as an attack. It will probably be the start of a massive fight versus the one who is very secure with themselves; they will take this as an opportunity to better themselves to better the relationship.

You will hear me refer to this statement throughout this chapter spirituality has everything to do with connection, and the connection that makes spirituality strong is communication. Years ago, when I was growing up in the hood, we had a saying that said what's understood doesn't have to be discussed. Still, I don't know if that applies in relationships because I think even things that are understood, sometimes you need to hear the tonality in your partner's voice sometimes you need to see the body language that they use when expressing something even if you already know it and have a grip on it. Having this conversation means that you must become vulnerable, which is a weak spot for many people. We like to be ostentatious and pretend like we got it all together when the truth of the matter is none of us do. And if we are not careful, any one of us can become the participant of having our spirituality missing in action. We will be saying one thing with our mouths, but our behavior will be displaying something completely different.

I will use myself as an example. I am a Pastor; it is my profession to communicate with people based on the communication I have with God through his word and through my prayer time. Sometimes, if I can be transparent, my ability to hear from God becomes clouded because of life issues that I must deal with as a husband, father, entrepreneur, and grandfather. I have many people who depend on me to stay in the space where my spirituality or connection with God remains connected. The dangerous part about what I do is it just takes one time for me to be off, to miss what God is saying, and someone's life could utterly be destroyed because my connection is not intact. I must discipline myself and make myself spend time with God even when I do not want to. Because if we are going, being honest, it does not matter what relationship we are talking about; sometimes, you do not want to be bothered. As good as God has been to me and all of us, even sometimes my relationship with Him, who is my savior, my Lord, and my King, I choose to avoid when I do not feel like being bothered.

I am sure some are shocked to hear a pastor say that, but again the ability that God gives us to communicate with him and connect with him in a safe space enables me to make honest statements like this. One of the worst things to have to deal with is to be in a relationship where you cannot be open and express the Y factor that is the foundation of what the problem may be in the relationship. I can talk about my relationship with God with such transparency because there is no judgment and there is no abuse, and there is no backlash for me expressing how I feel; therefore, he and I can discover the Y factor. There must be a reason why there is a disconnect, and who better to find out what the disconnect is or why the disconnect is other than the person you are in a relationship with. But the relationship's culture must be safe, healing and nurturing, and becomes the catalyst by which the breach can be repaired. If this is not the case, get your boxing gloves out because it is about to be a problem.

Most people claim that they want their partners to be 100% honest with them, but I have come to find out that most people cannot handle honesty at that level. It sounds good in a passionate conversation but are you ready for your partner to get completely transparent in your presence and say something that may shock you, express some issues and feelings that they have that may blow your mind. I guarantee you this will happen, but if you are mature enough to handle what you hear, you will gain wisdom and information to help the relationship heal and recover.

Now let's deal with this from a different perspective, disconnections happen in relationships for several reasons. You feel your partners' spirituality is missing because someone else has the attention you used to have. I am learning that sometimes it's not that the spirituality is missing; it's just that you don't have access to where the spirituality is anymore. Time is the greatest Prophet. I know it will tell you the truth; whether you want to hear it or not, it is up to you to take heed and listen to it and hear the instructions time gives you without ever uttering a word. It is vital to discuss what opens a man to connect and what opens a woman to connection. I will provide this one for you ladies for free a man will connect with anyone that strokes his ego. He will spend time with anyone that makes him feel like he matters. Men are entirely different than women who will open to a connection wherever they feel secure at! Gentlemen, it will be exceedingly difficult for you to maintain a relationship with a woman when you are the source of her insecurity. She will never make you happy if you make her feel less than a Queen, and sometimes, we as men have all of these expectations from the woman that we are involved with and have yet to deal with the inadequacy's that we bring to the relationship and that needs to be dealt with as well.

Let's take it one more step further… could it be that spirituality is missing in the relationship because the two parties have grown apart? I believe that men will evolve at least seven times in their life and that means who I was when I was 17, I will not be at 37, and sometimes people have a way of not growing with you and not respecting the development that you have achieved through the process and sometimes they are dealing with the old you instead of recognizing the new you. How annoying is that???

I know for me, the older I get, the less tolerance I have for a lot of noise, and that may be conflicting for some people to believe because of what I do, me being a producer, songwriter, musician, and recording artist, I'm surrounded by noise all the time. When I'm not working, I have to have peace and quiet. Still, suppose you're looking at me as just a musician or just someone that's in the studio all the time and someone that is around a lot of noise all the time instead of exploring the other side of me. In that case, there will be a disconnect because I am an individual who refuses to do anything that makes me uncomfortable. And suppose there is no connection between the people that are around me and me. In that case, they will get offended by that change instead of appreciating that the peace that I look for and that I long for is an opportune time for us to converse. For us to share what is on each other's heart because that cannot be accomplished around a whole lot of noise and a whole lot of people, the older I get, I find the treasure of silence.

That is one of the things that happens when there is no communication in a relationship. These things should be the catalyst for growth turn into the things that destroy relationships because of a lack of understanding. The Bible even instructs us that getting an understanding while you are out making money while you are out pursuing your dreams while you are out becoming great. Getting to that bag, understand what it means to be in a selfless relationship to prefer others over yourself. You will be able to maintain connections at the next level.

This statement and this platform for change can easily be offensive if the individuals involved do not want to resolve it. I have learned that only two things can happen when you communicate with people, which are resistance or results. And if you are like me, I have a desire for results. I'm not too fond of opposition; I don't enjoy people not understanding when I'm talking to them. Most of all, I don't want people ever to think I'm speaking at them, so I have to make sure that there is a clear communication line between me and whoever I'm in a relationship with. I do not like leaving room for guessing or assumptions. They both lead to unnecessary uncertainties. I am a firm believer that clear communication will always produce clear understanding.

This leads me to believe because spirituality or a connection is missing in the relationship does not necessarily mean that it is missing in the person; it could just be the relationship. This is where a degree of difficulty will come in your decisions. If the spirituality is not missing from you or in you, you must decide whether this relationship is worth trying to save and preserve. Let me remind you again that spirituality represents connection and that connection can only be maintained through communication. If there is no communication and no connection, is the relationship worth trying to salvage at this point? This is where you must make decisions that will not be popular, but you have to do it for self-preservation.

For far too long, I have seen people stay in relationships that they know have come to an end, but they remain in something where they are no longer being fulfilled because of habitual behavior and certain comfort levels. And that is where the doorway to so many negative situations creep into relationships, and people end up getting hurt emotionally and, unfortunately, sometimes even physically.

Once you have discovered that there has been a break in connection with your relationship's spirituality, this is nothing to play with; it must be addressed, and it must be addressed quickly. I will be candid and say this is a highly uncomfortable conversation to have if there is no transparency culture in your relationship. I guarantee you this, though, going through this one time will prevent you from ever going through this again. This space and this part of relational dealings are such a heavy educational journey; the older you get, the less time you have to waste and understand the value of connections. You also understand the responsibility and the accountability of maintaining those connections. The truth of the matter is the maintenance of the connection in a relationship is never one-sided; it is something that both parties should keep with equal levels of interest and passion. It is always easy to play the blame game when this void is discovered in our relationships, but the truth of the matter is it takes two people to have a connection, not one, and at some point, we all must take accountability for the breach. You should never allow the blame to be placed on your shoulders, gentlemen it takes 2 to mess things up… you have to blame her and her best friend, LOLLOLL….

Let's look at one of the positive things that come from anyone in a relationship being able to make this statement. If you can sit down and make this observation about the absence of spirituality, AKA connection in your relationship, you are emotionally healthy. While this may be a painful thing, I believe it is an excellent indicator that you are still very much in touch with your feelings and understanding what real love is supposed to be. Sometimes we spend so much time focusing on the negative of a situation without observing the positive lessons that we can walk away from whatever we are going through.

Pain is something that provokes growth; you will never know how to identify a real Prince until you kissed a few frogs. I believe that what we consider to be losses in most cases are lessons. It is something for us to take away that will cause us to grow and prepare us to be the very thing that we need in our next relationship. Because if there is no hope of repairing or reconnecting with the person that we feel is missing their spirituality, we must be prepared to move forward and connect with someone whose spirituality is very present.

I ignore the people that say they do not mind being by themselves; they do not need anybody and do not want anybody. I do not believe that. When people say statements like that, it goes against the very intent of God. When you look at creation, you see God creating Adam; God looks at Adam, who is his prized creation, the one that he trusts enough to name every animal on the planet. He has a job and an assignment, but he does not connect with other human beings. In the 2ND chapter of the book of Genesis, in the 18th verse, God said it is not suitable for man to be alone. I will therefore make him a help meet that is suitable for him. So, it is possible to connect with someone that is not the correct individual. That is why it is so important that even when choosing a mate, its spiritual aspect is crucial. Proverbs has a passage of scripture in the 3rd chapter that says to "Trust in the Lord with all your heart lean not to your understanding in all your ways acknowledge him and he will direct your path'. People experience so much disconnect because they do not acknowledge God before making decisions two connect with people in an emotional relationship. I believe the first connection that we must maintain is our connection with God, who in turn gives us guidance and warning signs concerning the decisions we make in our day-to-day activities. If our lives' spirituality is missing with him, I can almost guarantee that your relationship with people will suffer the consequences.

Please do not limit this discussion to a religious gathering or a denominational group; these principles can be applied to every human being regardless of race, creed, or color. Some may call him Christ or God. Some may call him Mohammed or Allah; the truth is whatever you believe, or whoever you think your God to be, that is the way you are taught and built from an integral perspective on how to maintain connections. Again, I have made it abundantly clear that I believe a spiritual connection can only be maintained through communication and that communication With God is prayer. Prayer is not just something that you apply or practice when you get into a crisis. It must be a daily routine if the connection is going to be maintained. No communication means no connection. You will find yourself making decisions from an emotional place instead of an analytical one, which in most cases never ends well.

Someone may be reading this and ask, well, Pastor J, what is the lesson attached to this? I practice this daily in my life; whatever you want, you must become. When you are stating that someone's spirituality is missing, you are saying that there is no connection. They possibly may be displaying a pattern that they care more about things than people, especially your relationship. Therefore, when you can spot this in your relationship, I think this is a golden opportunity for you to become an example of what you want to see. Now, if you do this and you still don't see the change in your partner, here is where you must make a grown-up decision. And you must ask yourself, is this the type of relationship I want to remain in? In no way, shape or form am I advocating for people to break up, but I know that the older I get, the more I realize, the less time I have to waste on things and relationships that will remain unproductive. A wise Carpenter measures twice and cuts once because they understand that you have to move forward with no regrets after the cut.

Another lesson attached to this revelation is that maybe you have not been the easiest person to remain connected to. It is always easy to blame your partner, and I know I joked about it earlier in the chapter about it being her fault and her best friend's fault, but the truth of the matter is some men do not know how to maintain relationship connections either. We go far with the whole I am the head; I am the man philosophy instead of tapping into the power of partnership. I think that this is something that we must discuss in this chapter and shine the light on to maintain the healthy relationship that we all desire.

The power of agreement is something that we do not discuss enough as couples. When I do marriage counseling, I always have the couple come in and sit down in my office, grab a pin and a piece of paper and my instructions are the following… write down five things that you love about your spouse and five things that you cannot stand about them. Then I want you to take your chairs, face each other and discuss the items on your list. Can I tell you that 99% of the time, the couples always start with the things that they cannot stand about each other, and it gets so heated that we never get to the stuff on the list that they love about each other. This is an experiment or exercise that I used to prove my theory that we spend more time building relationships on negative than positive. While I believe with all my heart that both are necessary because for anything to have power, it must have a negative and a positive side; you will never go into a store and purchase a battery that has a negative and a negative! That battery will be dysfunctional, and there will be no power; there must be a negative and positive side to anything that will have power.

This issue right here can be the very reason why you are not the one who gets chosen. Men are not that complex, neither are we that complicated. There are a lot of amazing women that are sitting and asking why did he marry her and play me? This is one of the reasons why men do not stay where there is no connection. For a man to even consider choosing you as the person, he will go into covenant with for the rest of his life and forsake all others and be true to you.

The expectation for that level of commitment to be maintained must be rooted and grounded in a spiritual connection in a safe space that the man feels that what he says and does is valued. If you think for one second that the way to maintain a spiritual connection with a man is by using what is between your legs, you have already set yourself up not to be chosen. Now he will play with you, he will have some fun with you, but he will never commit to you. Trust me while you are out buying negligees, new perfume, and candles from Bath and Body Works, sis down the street is sitting down listening to the heartbeat of your man listening to the vision plans that he wants to execute, and creating a space where he feels that he is heard and valued. Every man has a king and a fool inside of him; you will get whichever one you talk to the most.

The killer is this; you are probably better looking than she is and may even have a better shape than her. The key to not getting played is understanding that the most valuable thing you possess is not what's between your legs; it is your ability as a woman to make a man feel like he is a King. In no way, shape, or form, I suggest that sex does not create a connection in a relationship because it does. Still, I think we have made that the most important type of connection in our relationship for too long, and the truth of the matter is communication is. We must understand that both male and female parties can get sex from multiple places and multiple people anytime they choose but to find a space and a person that you can connect with from an intellectual standpoint is priceless. And once that is discovered, it is almost impossible to let go of.

I am what you call a sapiosexual, an individual turned on by the intellect before the physical. I enjoy engaging in conversations that appeal to my intelligence more than physical attraction. The older I get, the more I see this about myself and laugh at myself because it was not always this way. When I was a younger man, it was the direct opposite. I did not care about communication. All I cared about was the outside pulchritude and how good I would look with a particular type of young lady on my arm. But now that I am almost 50, I apply this principle to my marriage and all of my friendships. I find it difficult to be friends with people who do not know how to communicate verbally on a certain level. Most people who do not shift to another level in communication skills become challenging to engage with from a companion standpoint. I have no problem engaging with them from a teacher standpoint, but that is an entirely different conversation.

When spirituality is missing, it creates a void and opens the door for illegal connections. Because as afore stated, we were created to be relational. If we are going to function at our highest capacity, relationships must be maintained because both males and females seek that connection from another. Every human being was created with a need to worship something. Some people worship their money, worship their possessions, and worship God, but every one of us has been created with a need and a desire to worship something. This means that we must always make the culture in our relationships that allow for healthy dialogue and positive reinforcement. You may not always agree with one another, but you should always hear one another's heart.

When I was a little boy, my mom told me that you better do better now that you know better. After reading this book with all of this amazing information from all of these fantastic authors, I hope that you make these principles apply to your life in your relationships. We are all getting too old to make bad connections and remain in relationships that are not going anywhere. There is a popular saying amongst the young people, and I'm on team Yolo. While this may be a popular colloquialism, I understand the intended meaning behind it. You only live once, and guess what? This is not a dress rehearsal; this is the big stage and the big performance. So, if you are going to be in a relationship, strive to make sure that it is as healthy and productive as it can be from the foundation. We understand we cannot control who other people choose to be and what they choose to enroll in; we can only do that within ourselves. But we can be a shining example of what an individual with a healthy spiritual life looks like by how we communicate with our partners and, most of all, the way we communicate with God. This will ensure that your spirituality never will be M.I.A.

As I close this chapter, I want to share something that I find true; you will attract whatever it is that you respect. Could it be that you have drawn or connected with someone who's missing their spirituality because yours is missing? Grow in grace.

Contributing Author
Jason Williams

Jason Williams is a preacher, best-selling published author, inspirational speaker, musician, and businessman. With God's gifts, he has developed a way to use them to help others while maintaining the business side of things. He is a man of many talents, but his greatest desire is to see everyone that wants to win, win. He has a gift to influence and uses it to the best of his ability to steer people to God and their desires to succeed. There is no more incredible feeling than helping someone else see their dreams come true. He is currently working on a couple more endeavors to leave his mark on the earth.

CHAPTER TEN

Women Can Be Frogs Too

With
Jason Williams

In the old fairy tale, The Frog Prince, a prince in his past was in a bad relationship. While in that relationship, something transpired in his life that changed him for the rest of his life. The only way for him to return to his original form was to be kissed by his true love. Nowadays, there are so many ways we can take that particular story. But if you look at the situation, he was who he was until he met someone that changed him. One period of time, he was a Prince. He had resources; clearly, he had a future, but he is now living a life he never intended because of one relationship. He ended up having his life completely changed; his perspective completely changed. He was no longer the same man that he was because of that relationship.

How many of us can relate to this story? You were going along in life, and all was well, then pow things happened that caused you to see life from a perspective you didn't see before. If you have been in any relationship, this has happened. Most men may not want to admit it, but it happens. He could have been the committed sold-out one and the one he was sold out for cheated, and he then has no heart for anyone. Or vice versa, she was in love and wanted to spend the rest of her life with him, but he treated her like nothing, and now she is left with walls up to protect her heart. Now both people have trust issues. I said all that to set a precedence that most have had some things happen in our lives that we have to deal with and overcome if we have developed internal protective mechanisms. Whether it's some childhood family stuff or some relationship things that caused you trauma, you defend yourself from it, legit or not.

The problem comes when we see it in others but can't see it in ourselves. The way to overcome difficulties is first to admit there is one. You have to be willing to see your flaws and weaknesses so that you can address them respectively. I know it was his fault, and if he hadn't done this or that, you would still be together. But have assessed what part you played in your relationship demise. Yes, he made some bad choices but was it all him.....NO. Let's peel back a couple of layers of this to see what we come up with.

Ladies, we will walk through some turbulent waters, but if you hear me, it may surprise you. So, most of the women I know have these ideologies of what their perfect man is. Some even have lists of what they feel is most appropriate for them. The thing is, most, not all, of the prerequisites are due to some damage or hurt that was done to them previously and now has adjusted some of their perspectives on what the next guy is supposed to look like on paper. Do you realize that man will never exist, or at least not for you?

Why, you ask? Because this new guy that comes has to now make up for the last guy's situation. He now has to be extra careful and walk on eggshells to break down your walls and obstacles to purposely put him in the same category as the last guy. And the sad part is he doesn't even know it. He thinks he can be himself, but as soon as something looks like the other guy, your defense mechanism kicks in, and he is left trying to figure out how now to maneuver around that part of you if he sees you as his future. Now don't get me wrong, there are plenty of men who can recognize this and fight for what they want. They will stand strong to cut through the layers of hurt you have to get to the core of who you are. But how many good men walked away saying it's too much to deal with? Ladies, just because you think you have gotten over some stuff doesn't mean you have. Make sure you have been completely healed from the last situationship so you can move freely into another without dragging all those bags in looking for someone to help you unpack them.

Now I know some of you are saying this is a two-way street, and it is. There are some men with the same issues that need to be dealt with, and on both sides, true healing needs to occur. You may want this type, but the kind you need isn't that. We all would like the perfect package inside and out, but the reality is sometimes the most incredible person for you comes in an unexpected package that you would never know if you don't open it. We have to be willing to explore people for who they are, and you might find the diamond you have been searching for. Often, it appears that the men are under the pressure of women to live up to the standard women have set for them, but the women themselves don't live that same standard. How does your list require so much from him but so little from you? How are your standards so high, and yet you by yourself live beneath them? I understand as little girls the prince coming on a white horse to whisk you away to a happily ever after is a fairytale, but it's just a fairytale.

You can have great expectations when you live up to your expectations. You can have high expectations when you currently live at that level. But if you are working your way to that level, how can you look at someone on your level as beneath you. He may be working just like you to get there and right now struggling just like you. I will say this, and I hope it doesn't offend, but most men and women are more alike than they are different. Men process the world one way and women another. On that alone creates its own discussions. But when you throw in the past relationship piece, it becomes a whole other animal. Everyone is not meant to be together, and sometimes we look for an intimate relationship from someone who was only ever meant to be a friend. Yes, I believe you should be friends first, but you also need to know yourself enough to know when something doesn't work instead of making it work and forcing California into Maine. It won't work. I've seen plenty of relationships where everyone on the outside tells you both should go your separate ways, but they keep going through cycles trying to hold together something that should be let go of.

Ladies, stop trying to make something work that won't. Actions speak louder than words and if they show you one thing and say another, believe what you see. People can only do to you what you allow. If you allow certain things for so long, you teach people how they can treat you. Every relationship takes work and growth. If you want the perfect person, then be open and honest about who you are and allow them the grace to be open about who they are. Most successful relationships come from two people who know who they are and know their significant other. They allow each other to grow into the perfect person for their relationship. I hope you noticed that I said the ideal person for their relationship and not the person.

The reason for that is because if I am perfect for you now, what happens when you grow and change as time progresses. The one thing we all will do is change. We will have different thoughts; we will become physically different, emotionally different, and ideologically diverse. But if you were perfect for me ten years ago and didn't grow with me, then ten years later, we are at odds again. So, you must develop yourself to be adaptable in your relationship and allow your partner to grow and support that growth. A lot of long-term relationships don't work because someone doesn't want to grow. They want things to remain the same and not change. Change in the right direction should be inevitable and welcomed. We all will, and if you are looking for that forever person, you have to expect it and embrace it. That this is who I am, stuff only works for so long.

Now I would like to bring up a more sensitive topic. The princess ideology, yes, I said the princess ideology. The idea that every woman is a princess and should be treated as such. I do believe as a man we should treat all women with respect and chivalry. But everything doesn't bow to you. There is a level of balance that should exist in a relationship. I despise the statement "happy wife happy life" because it suggests that everything else is better for everyone else if she is happy. That is the furthest thing from the truth. A relationship consists of two people looking to serve the other. Yes, I said to serve. If all of my attention is to service your needs and all of your attention is to service my needs, how is there any issue? The issues come when one doesn't feel needs are being met and begins to resent their part in committed service to the other. No one is perfect, and the only way to find that perfect person is to allow yourself room to find someone willing to give themselves to the study of you as you give yourself to the study of them. Yes, women, as much as you may believe it, you are not perfect, and neither is he. But if you want to make things great, each has to give up something sometime for the sake of the relationship.

Relationships thrive on finding common ground where there are differences of opinions or beliefs. Even if the common ground accepts the other side as it is without the need to change them. The worst feeling in the world is to feel like you have made changes in your life for someone who doesn't seem to notice or that it seems never to be enough. I heard something recently that made me think. Women today want a man to treat them as the men treated women back in the day, take out the trash, get gas, fix things, wash cars, the "men things," but yet want the feminist movement and everything equal with men. Now hear me out before you jump to conclusions. You want your man to treat you like your grandfather treated your grandmother, but are you willing to treat your man like your grandmother treated your grandfather. Back then, there were gender roles, and in most successful relationships, each played their part. But it seems some of these women today want gender roles for men and none for women. How do you as a woman know what a man's supposed to do, but not what you should be doing to get what you want? Men want to feel wanted and needed too. We may not express it as you do, but we would like to get our wants and needs met if we do the things you express. All men aren't dogs, and all women aren't selfish.

We all have to want to give ourselves to our significant other so that they will be filled with the love they need instead of the love we offer. Yes, I said it that way purposely. Sometimes we offer love the way we see it and not the way it's needed. Hear your significant other's heart and be that instead of thinking if it were me, I would like it. They aren't you, and they may accept it but won't like it. We have to understand that our expression of love toward one another needs to be communicated in a way that is fulfilling to our significant other. Not just something but something that resonates with them to show we listen to their wants and needs.

ALL women are not princesses. ALL men are not Frogs. When we accept people for who they are and what they bring to the table, we are less likely to fall for the counterfeits. If I see you for who you are and not what you project, I can make better decisions about whether we fit together. The primary issue does you accept the other for what they show you. In the story, the frog was not precisely what you saw. And when his environment was conducive for him to be his entire self, he was able to do so. So, what type of atmosphere are you creating for your significant other? Are they being nurtured to be their best selves, or are they what it is they are forced to project because the environment they're in only accepts a specific type?

The Frog Prince teaches us the value of keeping your word and being committed to the promise you made. But if we begin this story with misinformation, there is nothing that you can do to appease someone. But if both parties are candid with who they are and are committed to service to each other, the service efforts will create the atmosphere for each person to be ultimately themselves. This allows the relationship to be all they need, and then the fairytale you wanted will become a reality.

The

End

For Now!